TOURISM INDUSTRY IN GUJARAT

SANJAYKUMAR D. PARAMAR
JAGDISHBHAI A. PARMAR

Canadian Academic Publishing
2013

First Edition : 2013

ISBN : 978-0-9921651-8-5

Publisher ISBN Prefix : 978-0-9921651

ISBN Allotment Agency : Library and Archives Canada (Govt. of Canada)

Canadian Academic Publishing
81, Woodlot Crescent,
Etobicoke,
Toronto, Ontario, Canada.
Postal Code- M9W 6T3
Phone- +1 (647) 633 9712
http://www.canadapublish.com

ACKNOWLEDGEMENT

We would like to thank our family members as well as our colleagues who have inspired us to write down this book.
We have immense pleasure to dedicate this book to

1. Dr. D.G.Ganvit

2. Dr. Manoj R Patel

3. Prof. Gaurang Desai

They have provided their precious blessing for the publication of book.

CONTENT

CONTENT

CHAPTER – I
TOURISM IN INDIA

Introduction

Tourism is the most important industry in the service sector of the Indian economy. It is one of the world's fastest growing industry and it can play role in accelerating the economic development of the country is widely recognised. It has generated a number of social and economic benefits, promotes national integration and international understanding, creates employment opportunities to a large number of people and foreign exchange earnings. Tourism also supports local handicrafts and cultural activities. For many developing countries, particularly the small country. They are mainly dependent upon tourism; this tourism offers a more reliable source of income

Number of factors, such as, population growth, shorter working days, larger paid holidays, increase in general awareness among people for traveling and the need for recuperation from tensions of modern life, have created favorable conditions for the growth of tourism. So this industry has registered a tremendous growth all over the world during the last few years.

Over the years, tourism has emerged as a major segment of the Indian economy, contributing substantially to the foreign exchange earnings and creating large-scale employment opportunities. Various aspects of the development of tourism in our country are briefly reviewed below.

Tourism Policy of Government

Tourism in country really came of age when the national policy began laying stress on the sector from the Third Five Year Plan during which the plan outlay for developing tourism was raised to RS. 8.00 crores from a mere Rs. 1.58 crores during the Second Five Year Plan. Increasing public sector outlays have been allocated to tourism during the successive five-year plans, Rs. 195 crores during the Sixth Plan and Rs. 345 crores during the Seventh Plan[1]. The outlay for the Eighth Plan period has been fixed at a substantially higher level of Rs. 804.10 crores[2].

A tourism policy was formulated and presented to Parliament for the first time only In November 1982. This policy was, unfortunately, more a statement of purpose than a concrete plan, which was operationalised. The Sixth Plan

1

document spelt out the objectives of the tourism but it was far from being a comprehensive policy document or an action plan for the development or promotion of tourism in the country. The Seventh Plan outlined a long-term perspective on the development of tourism. It also advocated granting industry status to tourism, clear demarcation of the roles of the private and public sector and encouragement of investment in the public sector exploiting tourism potential to support the local arts and handicrafts sector and to promote national integration.

A significant milestone in the evolution of a tourism policy was the comprehensive report presented by the National Committee on Tourism in May 1988, which provided the basis of a long-term perspective plan for tourism .

During the Seventh Plan several new policy initiatives were taken to develop the tourism sector on an accelerated growth path. Tourism was accorded the status of an Industry. At present, 15 states and 3 Union Territories have declared tourism as an Industry. In addition, four states have declared hotels as an Industry[4]. Consequently, a number of incentives have been provided to private entrepreneurs for investment in tourism activities. The future growth, of tourism will be achieved through private initiative. The state can contribute to tourism by planning broad strategies of development, provision of fiscal and monetary incentives to catalyze private sector Investments and devising effective regulatory and supervisory mechanism to protect the interest of the industry, the consumer and the environment.

In the Eighth Plan, the "Special Tourism Areas" concept is being adopted, wherein a few tourist areas with high tourism potential will be identified and provided with full-fledged infrastructure facilities

Organizations Involved in Tourism
The various organisations engaged in the development of tourism are

I) Department Of Tourism
It is responsible for promotion of India as a tourist destination, development of tourism Infrastructure and facilities in the country, and performing regulatory functions in the field of tourism. It has four regional offices at Delhi, Mumbai, Kolkata, and Chennai and a sub-regional office at Guhawati. The regional offices supervise the working of other tourist offices situated at different places throughout the country. Tourist offices are also located at various places abroad.

ii) India Tourism Development Corporation (ITDC). It was established In October 1966. Its activities include;
• Construction, management and marketing of hotels, restaurants and travelers lodges at various places in the country;
• provision of tourist publicity materials;
• Provision of entertainment facilities in the shape of sound and light shows, music concerts, etc.,
• Provision of shopping facilities in the shape of duty free shops; and
• Provision of consultancy-cum-managerial service in India and abroad.
The Corporation had 31 hotels / travelers lodges with 3762 rooms at the end of 1990-91.

iii) Indian Institute of Tourism and Travel Management (ITTM).

It was set up in January 1983 with registered office at New Delhi. It offers different level academic courses in tourism and travel management and related areas. It has embarked upon a series of alternative educational courses for supervisory and grass root-level workers of the Industry. Universities in 20 developing countries are sending their faculty members for being trained in IITTM courses.

iv) National Council for Hotel Management and Catering Technology.

It acts as an apex body to coordinate training and research in hotel and catering management. Its head office is In New Delhi. It is the main agency for planning and monitoring the activities of 15 Institutes of Hotel Management and 15 Food Craft Institutes end ensures uniformity in academic standards and procedure for selection and admission of candidates for various courses conducted by these institutes.

v) Tourism Finance Corporation of India Ltd. (TFCI).

This Corporation, sponsored by the Industrial Finance Corporation of India, was set up In April 1988 with Initial seed capital of Rs. 50 crores to provide institutional assistance to tourism projects other than those in the accommodation sector, as the Industrial Finance Corporation of India at concessional rate of Interest was financing these. It started its operations from 1-2-1989.

In addition to the above mentioned organisations at the Central level, the State governments and Union territories have their own Departments of Tourism, Tourism Development Corporations and other Institutions or organisations formed for the purpose of helping the development of tourism industry in their areas. Besides this institutional support, a large number of other agencies, such as the Department of Archaeology, International Airport Authority of India, Indian Airlines, Vayudoot, Indian Railways, Customs Department, Reserve Bank of India, Forest Departments, Handloom and Handicrafts Boards and Corporations and Individual travel agents, hotels and tour operators are engaged in the promotion of tourism in India.

Growth of Tourism

As evidenced by the following data, tourism industry has recorded a substantial growth in India over the years.

i) Foreign Tourist Arrivals

The large number of tourists are visiting India from various countries.

The number of foreign tourists who came to India increased from 17,000 in 1951 to 1.71 million In 1990[6]. In fact, the foreign tourist arrivals have crossed the one million mark In 1986 when the country received 10,80,000 foreign tourists. But it was not a spectacular achievement considering the fact that it formed just 0.4 per cent of the global tourist traffic in that year. As stated by the then Civil Aviation and Tourism Minister Mr. Madhavrao Scindia in the Rajya Sabha, on November 24,1992, the number of foreign tourists who visited India during 1991 was 16,77,508. This shows a decline in the foreign tourist arrivals in the country in 1991, as compared to that in the previous year, though 1991 was declared as the 'VISIT INDIA YEAR'. Thus, the target of receiving 2.5 million tourists by the end of the Seventh Five Year Plan could not be achieved. What is more disappointing is the fact that the already poor share of the country in the global tourist traffic declined further from 0.4 percent In 1986 to 0.35 per cent in 1990. It looks rather ironical in view of the fact India, with her colourful geographical features, unique historical and cultural mosaic, fascinating fauna and flora, sun-drenched bathing beaches, majestic rivers, glorious architecture and beautiful and sublime literature, has inexhaustibly attractive tourism resources. It is anticipated that tourist traffic will grow at the rate of 9 to 10 per cent per annum and about 2.75 million tourist will visit India by the end of the Eighth Plan.

4

Table 2.1 Arrivals of Foreign Tourist

Year	Arrivals
1991	1677508
1992	1867651
1993	1760418
1994	1886433
1995	2123683
1996	2287860
1997	2374094
1998	2358623
1999	2471848
2000	2624259

(Source) Department of tourism annual report 2001.

Above table indicate the data related to arrival of tourist in India According to the data, every year it should increasing trends in last decade. In 1991, 1677508 tourist have visited India, and 2624259 tourist have been visited India during 2000.

India's top 10 tourist markets are the U.K., the U.S.A., F.R.G. (erstwhile), France, Japan, Shri Lanka, Italy, Canada, and U.S.S.R. and Malaysia, in the order of importance . But three countries - the U.K., the U.S.A. and Germany (East and West combined) contribute the lion's share or tourist arrivals in India. They accounted for 14.9 per cent, 11.6 per cent and 6.0 per cent respectively of the total number of tourists who visited India In 1986 • Hence, it is imperative to make all possible efforts to attract tourists from other European and South-east Asian countries and from the Middle East.

ii) Foreign Exchange Earnings

Tourism in India has emerged as the largest net foreign exchange earner, Its contribution to the foreign exchange earning of the country increased from a meager Rs. 32 crores in 1974-75 to more than Rs. 3000 crores[9] (Rs. 3318 crores as per the aforesaid statement of Shri Madhavrao Scindia in the Rajya Sabha on November 24, 1992). Since Imports of goods needed for tourism are limited, value added component in terms of foreign exchange earning of this industry is relatively high. India spends only 7 cents to earn a dollar from tourism, while the costs of earning one dollar from gems and jewellery and engineering goods are

70 cents and 40 cents, respectively[10]. But India's foreign exchange earnings from tourism are a paltry figure when compared to some other countries. For example, in 1980, India earned dollar 603 million from tourism as compared to dollar 1,317 million earned by a tiny country like Hong Kong[11]. In 1991, our country earned a mere 0.6 per cent of dollar 230 billion international spending on tourism[12]. The National Committee on Tourism had estimated that foreign exchange earning from tourism could be increased to about Rs. 5000 crores by the year

Table 2.2 Earning of Foreign Exchange

Year	Earning of Foreign Exchange
1991	3589.90
1992	5781.87
1993	6304.98
1994	7116.24
1995	8437.41
1996	9714.61
1997	10482.38
1998	11280.45
1999	12175.97
2000	14408.63

(Source) Department of Tourism Annual Report 2001 2000 A.D., at 1986-87 prices.

Table 2.2 indicate the data regarding foreign earnings during last 10 years of country. After Globalisation process, this earnings has been increased. It was 3589.90 during 1991 and highest 14408.63 during 2000.

(iii) Employment Generation

Being a labour intensive Industry, tourism has immense potential for generating employment, particularly for the educated unemployed. By the rule of thumb, one additional tourist from an affluent country creates one more job in India, for a foreign tourist spends Rs.18, 000 during his stay in the[13] country on an average . The expenditure by tourists has a multiplier effect on employment. According to the Tata Economic Consultancy Services Report of 1982, for every job created by tourism sector 2.57 jobs were created elsewhere. The multiplier effect of tourism in terms of employment generation is clearly indicated by the fact that out of 4.5 million persons engaged in this industry in India in 1988, 1.5 million persons were directly employed[14]. In 1991, 5.3 million people were directly related to the tourism industry and another 13.8 million Indirectly[15].

Tourism is a basic industry which provide employment. In India Jammu and Kashmir is completely depending on tourist arrival

Table 2.3 Direct Employment by Indian Tourism Industry

Year	Direct Employment
1990-91	5500000
1995-96	8500000
1996-97	9100000
1997-98	9900000
1998-99	10700000
1999-2000	11500000
2000-01	12500000
2001-02	13500000
2002-03	14500000
2003-04*	15700000
2004-05*	17000000
2005-06*	18300000

So the economy can developed, sub area of economical activities like, Hotels, Transports, Telephones, Caterings, Food processing, Local handy Craft, so this sector can generate large number of opportunities and possibilities for growth of social sector. Good road-highway, hotels, telecommunication, Restaurant etc. tourism related sectors which can be growth according to the growth of this sector.

Table No.2.3 indicate the data above direct employment by Indian Tourism industry. It shows increasing trends every year. So this industry can play its important role in economical and social developments.

iv) Provision of Accommodation

The growth of tourism can also be measured in terms of the availability of hotel rooms, one of the most important infrastructure facility needed for the industry, in the country. The number of approved hotels and their rooms, in the country, increased from 186 and 7,085 in 1963 to 694 and 44,405 respectively in 1990[16]. But the rooms available have been falling short of the demand for them. In 1988, the country was short of accommodation by at least 25,000 rooms,

According to Mishra, secretary; ministry of tourism, while addressing the International Tourism Council (ITC) on April 30, 1988 (reported in The Economic Times, Bombay, dated May 1, 1988)*. The National Committee on Tourism In its report has foreseen a requirement for one-lakh rooms in the various categories. However the Union Minister for Tourism and Civil Aviation Shri Scindia has told on August 8, 1992 (The Economic Times, Bombay, August 26, 1992) that the number of hotel rooms will be doubled within three years.

Table 2.4 Star Hotel in India

Year	Fivestarhotel	Total star hotel
1990	15000	44000
1991	15000	44000
1992	15700	47000
1993	16000	51000
1994	18000	55000
1998	19610	64573

(Source) Facts for you July 1997 p.35

* Above table indicate the information above availability of hotels. In 1990, 15000 rooms were available in five star hotels and 44000 rooms were available in total stars (industry every star hotels) hotel. This is increased in 1998

Problems of Tourism Industry

The foregoing analysis of the growth of tourism in India shows that although the industry has registered an all round substantial development in the country during the last two-three decades, most of the potential, for its growth has not yet been exploited and much more is left to be desired. The limited, and rather unsatisfactory, growth of this industry in our country has been due to a number of problems it is beset with and various difficulties it has been facing. The important factors, which have limited the growth of tourism in India, are mentioned below:

• Inadequate airline capacity, particularly during the peak tourist season, bad conditions of our airports, delays in getting the bookings, flight cancellations and delays render air travel in India nightmarish for foreign tourists.

• Due to appalling conditions of traveling by trains, in India tourists prefer to avoid unless unavoidable.

• Lack of hygienic and comfortable accommodation for the tourists, in general, but reasonable good accommodation for low spending middle class tourists in particular, render tourism unattractive. Absence of motel hampers the smoothness, of long distance travels.

• There is absence of an up to date information systems with quick retrieval facilities causes inconvenience to tourists.

• Another major factor inhibiting the growth of tourism is the seasonality of the industry with the busy season being limited to six months from October to March and heavy rush in November and December.

• Lack of an integrated tourism promotion programme during the five-year plan periods has hindered the growth of tourism.

• Indifference of many states and union territories to tourism, which has not yet been accorded industry status by them, is another factor limiting its growth.

• Next factor is the failure of the mandarins of tourism to quickly adopt to the changing environment, for example the temporary closure of Jammu and Kashmir to tourists and socio-political and religious agitations in other northern states of the country rendering them unattractive to tourists, by developing and promoting alternative tourists destinations in South India.

• A lukewarm attitude towards the domestic tourism due to the emphasis placed by the authorities on foreign tourism has been another limiting factor. We should not forget that domestic tourists have its own importance and its development provides a sound basis for the growth of international tourism.

After a brief discussion of the problems and difficulties faced by tourism in India and the factors limiting its growth in the country, the researcher have studied by the various measures taken by the government recently for prompting tourism have been discussed below.

Measures Taken for Promotion of Tourism :

The Central and the State governments and their concerned agencies or departments for the development of tourism in India have taken a number of measures. Some important steps taken recently in this regard are as under:

- To promote India as a destination of 1990s, 18 Extension Circuits have been identified for development. These circuits specifically relate to adventure, wildlife, winter and water sports and beaches. In order to encourage water sports and to bring professionalism in the field, a National Institute of Water Sports has been set up in Goa for developing pilgrimage tourism 21 places have been selected in the country.
- To help the ITDC to attract more foreign tourists it has been decided to allow it to have marketing and management development collaborations with M/s. Radisson Hotel Corporation of U. S. A.
- With a view to bring in foreign exchange and generate funds for modernisation of ITDC run hotels, the union civil aviation and tourism ministry has decided to privatise these hotels. The first basket of hotels proposed to be privatised were those in Delhi, Udaipur, Jaipur, and Aurangabad. The proposal was to disinvest 40 per cent of the equity to the international hotel chains, 20 per cent to the hotel employees and financial institutions and retain the remaining 40 with the government. This has irked the Indian hoteliers who have been sidetracked.
- The Central government has assisted State government to set up inexpensive accommodation at important tourist centers for the Yatri Niwases.
- In 1988, 50 per cent of foreign exchange earnings of hotels and travel agencies were made tax-free straightaway. The Government of India has allowed upto 51 per cent foreign participation in hotel industry. Further, a tax rebate of 25 per cent of profits up to a period of eight years for approved hotel, which commenced operations between March 31, 1981 and April 1, 1990, has also been announced. Under the "Equity Scheme", which became operative from April 1992, the Central Department of Tourism ad the State government will contribute to the equity capital of tourism ventures

- The budget of 1992-93 has raised the lower limit of single room tariff from Rs.400 per night to Rs.1200 for levying of 20 per cent Hotel Expenditure Tax. However, the tourism and civil aviation ministry has recommended to the finance ministry withdrawal of this tax. Partial convertibility of the rupee, abolition of duty on cars used as taxi from 230 per cent to 175 per cent, are some other steps included in the budget in this direction.
- On July 6, 1992, India and Israel signed a protocol on promoting tourism between the tow countries by facilitating travel and cooperating in joint promotion of tourism from third countries, wherever feasible.
- With a view to attract more foreign tourists during the lean season, Air India, Indian Airlines and ITDC and some other hotel chains have joined hands and evolved a summer package called " Super-Saver Package " consisting of 11 itineraries of seven days stay India whit an option for four days extension and based on attractive rates.
- In order to automatically inform the passengers on telephone the revised departure timings of substantially delayed flights, known two hours or more in advance, a computerised facility called " Real time Automatic Passenger Information Dissemination System (RAPID)" has already been introduced in Delhi and was opened in Chennai at the Indian Airlines Offices, on April 13, 1992.
- In addition to the " Palace on Wheels a special tourists train comprising meter gauge " Vintage Saloons " which started taking the tourist through Rajasthan from January 26, 1982, it has been decided to flag off tourist train, " Temple on Wheels " which will cover different places in Karnataka and Goa in an itinerary of six days.
- Appointment of a committee by the Ministry of Environment under the chairmanship of Mr. B. B. Vohra, in March 1992, to suggest modifications in coastal regulations for setting up of hotels and other tourism facilities near beaches is another important step for boosting up tourism.
- Opening of Ladakh for foreign tourists, lifting of the restrictions on the operation of chartered flights to India and reduction in visa fees are some other steps taken recently to attract tourists to India.

Table 2.5 Arrival of Foreign Tourist in World Tourism (in lacks) * Expected

Year	Arrivals of Foreign Tourist
1950	253
1960	693
1965	1127
1970	1597
1975	2151
1980	2800
1984	3000
1997	6130
1999	6570
2000	6610
2010*	9370
2020*	15610

(Source) Nation Council on Tourism Ahmedabad. Date: 18/2 /2000.

Above table no. 2.5 reveals data about total number of foreign tourist visited India from 1450 and expected to visit till to the 2020. It is expected that passenger will come regularly in various parts of the country.

Table 2.6 Daily Average Cost of Tourist Year 1998

Name of the Country	Cost in Dollar
India	52.8
Corea	221.0
China	198.5
Philipines	12704

(Source) National Seminar on tourism Ahmedabad
Dated 18-2-2000.

Table 2.6 indicate the very important information about average of daily stay in various countries. It indicate that the average cost of living per day in India is lowest were as it is highest highest in philipines. So it is favorable situation for marketing strategy of the nation.

Conclusion

Apart from the aforesaid measures taken by the Central Government, the State Governments too have taken different steps and started various schemes within their areas for the development of tourism. Some as listed below.

• Exemption of buildings constructed for the development of tourism from the payment of building tax by the Government of Kerala.
• Identification of 254 ancient buildings as heritage hotels by the tourism department Rajasthan.
• Approval of the investment of Rs. 28 crores for setting u nine hotels in Tamil Nadu by the State Government in April 1992.
• A master plan for development of beach tourism as Puri and Konark drawn up by the Orissa Government.
• Selection of Hardwar, Varanasi, Ayodhya, Mathura and Badrinath under the scheme of developing five major pilgrim places as centres of tourism by the Government of Uttar Pradesh.
• Scheme of Maharashtra Tourism Development Corporation for the development of 34 historic forts in Maharashtra as tourist centers, and
• The proposal of West Bengal Government to develop Sunderbans as a major tourist attraction is a few examples of such measures.

The foregoing review of the tourism industry in India leads us to the conclusion that although substantial growth has been recorded by it in our country, there is a great potential, which could not be exploited on account of inadequate infrastructure facilities. Hence, there is an imperative need for further improving the country's tourism infrastructure including accommodation, transport, information and communication facilities.

Tourism is a product-cum service that requires continuous trimming, moderation and up dating in a fiercely competitive international environment. Effective marketing is the key to the problems of development of tourism for which a detailed analysis of the market profiles of India's main tourism generating regions is required. Aggressive marketing will have to be taken up in the existing tourism generating markets abroad as well as to explore new markets. Simultaneously, all-out efforts should be made for the development of the domestic tourism, which would serve as a sound ground for the growth of foreign tourism. Proper cooperation and coordination between the public and the private sector is a must for the future growth of tourism in the country. Further, there is a need for greater coordination among the adjoining states having tourist places of international significance. It could be in terms of inter-state tours with the help of common fleet of all India permit luxury buses.

Following data previous information about development of tourism consider legal structure of the country. It was not enough, government has to do more things for the growth of the Indian Tourism.

Year	Particulars
1946	Sir John Sarjant Committee on Tourism
1947	Report of sir John Committee
1949	Sir John Committees Suggestions, Government Started branches of tourism in Delhi, Culcatta, Bombay and Madras.
1951-55	First five year plan, No allotment for tourism Development
1956-60	Allotment for tourism with name of transportation Division
1957	Establishment of Department of tourism
1958	Establishment of Tourism Department council
1960	Establishment of Indian Tourism Development corporation (ITDC)
1966	Establishment of Department of Aviation
1966	Establishment of Department of Aviation and Tourism
1967	Establishment of Ministry of tourism and civil Aviation
1982	Declared First time tourism policy
1986	Establishment of National Committee on tourism
1986	Separate Department of Tourism
1986	Tourism as a Industry Declared by Government
1986	Separate Department with Cabinet Minister

1988	Establishment of Ministry of Civil Aviation Tourism
1991	Tourism as a Sources of Foreign Investment
1992	National action plan for tourism
1992	Tourism year
1995	Establishment of tourism cell
1988-99	Tourism with export businesses
1999-2000	Visit India year
2002	The concept of highway tourism, agricultural tourism, and rural tourism.

Above table reveals account shift in thinking process of the government

It is high time the concerned authorities realised that the growth of tourism is a necessity and not a luxury and a pre - requisite for assuring adequate foreign exchange earnings to maintain the tempo of economic development of the country. It would be in fitness of the things to recognise International tourism as an export Industry. But in our pursuit of foreign tourism promotion we should not forget its severe limitations and inherent dangers. We should, simultaneously, guard against environmental degradation and not allow the local people, culture and traditions to be swamped by foreign tourists.

References

1. Naik S.D., Belied Expectations, Missed opportunities, Midweek Review, Hotels and Tourism, The Economic Times, Mumbai, dated March 19, 1991.
2. Government of India, Planning Commission, New Delhi, Eighth Five Year plan 1992-97, Vol.1., p.54.
3. Zaidi, Madhu Suri, Tourism, A Wealth of Potential, Sadly Unrealised, The Economic Times, Mumbai, dated March 51991.
4. Government of India, Planning Commission, New Delhi,
5. Eighth Five Year Plan 1992-97, Vol.II, p. 253,
6. Seth, P., The Travails of Tourism Industry, The Economic Times, Mumbai dated March 5, 1991.

7. Chander, Navika, Promises to Keep and Miles to Go, The Economic Times, Mumbai, Mid-Week Review, Tourist Trade, dated February 11, 1988.
8. Eighth Five Year Plan, Vol.II Op. cit., p. 253.
9. Seth, P. The Travails of Tourism Industry, 0p. cit.
10. 11.Ruchika, Key to Exchange Earnings, Mid-Week Review, Tourist Trade, The Economic Times Mumbai, dated
11. Seth, P. The Travails of Tourism industry, Op. cit,
12. 14.Datt, Narayan, By the End of 2000 A.D., Mid-week Review, Tourist Trade, The Economic Times, Mumbai, dated
13. 15. Sanjgiri, Vasant Hotel Industry, - "Promoter of Economic Development, Mid-week Review, Hotels and Tourism, The Economic Times, Mumbai, dated September 19, 1991.

CHAPTER – II
TOURISM IN GUJARAT

Introduction

In recent years tourism has emerged as a major economic activity that is employment oriented and earns foreign exchange. Its share in the World's GDP in 1994-95 was 10%, which is more than the world military budget put together. In global terms, the investment in tourism industry and travel trade accounts for 7% of the total capital investment. Today 21.2 crore people around the globe are employed in travel trade and tourism. In future, this is likely to see unprecedented growth. According to the World Tourism Council of Brussels, (1) The revenues from travel and tourism in Asia-Pacific region will grown at the rate of 7.8% annually over the next decade.

Amongst the economic sectors the tourism sector is highly labour intensive. A survey by the government of India notes that the rate of employment generation(direct and indirect) in tourism is 52 persons employed per Rs.10m lakh investment (based on 1992-93 consumer price index). This is much higher than the rates of employment generation in most other economic sector.

India's tourism industry has also recorded phenomenal growth. The rate of international arrivals in India in recent years has been to the tune of about 19 lakh arrivals per year. The unprecedented growth in tourism in India has made it the third largest foreign exchange earner , after gem and jewellery and readymade garments .This is not surprising since India possesses a whole range of attractions normally sought by tourists and which includes natural attractions like landscapes, scenic beauty, mountains, wildlife, beaches, rivers and manmade attractions such as mountain forts, palaces and havelis. However, in global terms, in spite of such attractions, tourist arrivals in India a mere 0.30% or the world arrivals. Receipts are similarly low, just a 0.50% of the world receipts. We are still quite far from the target of 50 lakh tourists arrivals per year.

Tourism in Gujarat

A separate Tourism Department was established in 1973 to identify and develop the tourism potential in the state. This was followed by the creation of Tourism Corporation of Gujarat in 1978, which was entrusted with the task of undertaking and developing tourism-related commercial activities. The corporation is presently engaged in a variety of activities such as creation of lodging and boarding facilities for the tourists and other aspects of tourists facilitation such as transportation packaged tours, wayside catering along the National and State highways, arranging cultural festivals, organizing exhibitions and producing and distributing maps, posters brochures and pamphlets. The corporation has set up accommodation facilities at Chorwad, Ahmedpur Mandvi, Porbandar, Veraval, Hajira, Ubhrat and Tithal. Similar facilities as pilgrimage centers like Palitana, Somnath, Dwarka, Pavagadh and Dakor have also been setup by the corporation. One of the recent tourist attractions introduced by the corporations in collaboration with the Indian Railways is the special tourist train, " The Royal Orient Train " which connects up various tourist destinations straddling the Gujarat and Rajasthan State. However, the corporation has suffered losses due to a number of organizational constraints. In order to minimize these losses and also to provide better services to the tourists, the government has undertaken privatisation of some of the commercial property units of the corporation. In spite of possessing a variety of tourist attraction such as wildlife scenic beauty, pilgrimage centers, exotic traditional crafts and festivals, beaches, hospitality of the region and a varied and healthful and tasteful cuisine. The state has not been able to accelerate the pace of tourism in comparison to other states. In 1991, the state did declare a tourism policy but it did not elicit adequate response from the private sector since the policy contained only a handful of benefits, while the implementation was difficult due to legal and administrative constraints.

Table 3.1 Allotment Fund for the development of tourism

No	Year	Allotment of Rupee (In Lakh)	Change in Percentage (%)
1	1996-97	350	-
2	1997-98	350	-
3	1998-99	1300	271 %
4	1999-2000	2450	88.46 %
5	2000-2001	2925	19.38 %
Total		7375	

(Source) General administration Gujarat State Gandhinagar

Above table 3.1 data indicate the information about fund allocation for this Industry by the soneynment of buyamat. It is dear that till to the 1996-97 the fundallocation is low, but than after there is mereased by percent and than every year government has increased the amount for the tourism industry.

While other state governments made successful efforts in developing tourism within their states, the relative inability of the Gujarat State to harness and develop its full tourist potential may be attributed to a combination of factors such as lack of effective policies, inadequate infrastructure, ineffective marketing and a lack of decent facilities for the tourists.

The main rationale for formulating a comprehensive tourism policy is rooted on the one hand, in the convergence of socio-economic spread benefits, environment friendliness and employment potential of tourism industry and on the other hand, in the growing demand for tourism products in the state, brought by a rapid industrial growth in the state during the recent years that has led to tremendous increase in number of business travelers.

Objectives

The objectives of tourism policy of the state could be classified into main objective and other related objectives

Main objective

To undertake intensive and extensive development of tourism in the state and hereby increase employment opportunities.

Other related objectives are

* Identify and develop tourist destinations and related activities.
* Diversification of tourism products in order to attract more tourists through a varied consumer choice.
* Comprehensive development of pilgrimage centers as tourist destinations.
* Create adequate facilities for budget tourists.
* Strengthen the existing infrastructure and develop new one where necessary.
* Creation of tourism infrastructure so as to preserve handicrafts, folk arts and culture of the state and thereby attract more tourists.

Approach and Strategy

In addition to the facilitation role assigned to itself by the Government in the development of tourism, the Government will adopt the following strategy towards the private sector with the objective of securing its active involvement in leading the development of tourism in the state.

* The tourism will be given the status of industry in order that the facilities and benefits available to the industry are also made available to tourism projects.

* A special incentive packages will be made available for encouraging new tourism projects as well as expansion of existing tourism units.

* Infrastructure facilities will be strengthened and developed within the state, particularly in special tourism areas which will be notified later and which will be developed by adopting an integrated area.

* Effective mechanism will be set up to build meaningful co-ordination with the Central Government and the State Government agencies the local self-government bodies and the NGOs.

* Government will encourage building effective linkage with the relevant economic agents and agencies such as the national and international tour operators and travel agents of repute hotel chains and global institutions connected with tourism such as WTO.

Policy Proposal

Tourism is industry like other industrial projects, and it also involves professional management capital investment, special skills and training. The Government of India and a number of other states have declared tourism as an industry. Gujarat State which is at the forefront of the industrial development will also declare tourism as an industry. This will enable the tourism projects to be eligible to get benefits. Availability of land is primary requirement of any project. The process of grant of land will be facilitated in urban areas for the projects concerning setting up of hotels restaurants and apartment hotels etc..

Existing arrangements for grant of government waste land to industrial units will be made applicable to various tourism projects.

Arrangement will be made to acquire private land for various tourism projects by companies registered under the Companies Act.

The existing commercial rates of NA assessment applicable to land involving tourism projects would be reviewed and rates of NA purpose will be made applicable to them.

As infrastructure creating institutions, the State Financial Institutions have made an important contribution in creating conducive environment for industrial entrepreneurs. They will be called upon to do the same for tourism entrepreneurs in terms of making available adequate finance.

So far, the leading from the state financial institution has been largely confined to hotels only. In reality, the range of activities for tourism projects is far larger than just hotels as can be seen from the following illustrative list:

Accommodation projects
*   Hotels
*   Resorts
*   Motels
*   Apartment hotels
*   Heritage hotels
Food oriented projects
*   Restaurants
*   Way side facilities on the state highways

Other tourism related projects
*   Amusement parks and water sports
*   Handicraft village complexes
*   Fairs and festivals
*   Camps and facilities encouraging adventure
*   Train travel projects
*   Sea / River cruise project
*   Sound and Light Shows
*   Museums
*   Natural parks / zones
*   Safari projects
*   Rope-ways
*   Sports / Health facilities complexes
*   Training schools for the managerial expertise for hospitality industry
*   Golf courses

Service oriented projects
*   Travel agency
*   Tour operation
*   Transport operation
*   Linkage with the international hotel chains (Franchise)
*   Human Resources Development (HRD) for tourism industry and necessary training facilities.

Table 3.2

Types of Hotel No and Capacity of Room

No	Types of Hotel	No of Hotels	No of Room
1	Five star Delux	55	12948
2	Five Star	50	6654
3	Four star	79	6131
4	Heritage	62	1916
5	Three star	316	15590
6	Two star	324	11391
7	One star	146	5095
8	Other	197	8307
Total		1229	68032

(Source) Department of Tourism Annual Report 2000.

Above table gives clear cut idea about the capacity of rooms in the fine star deluxe and five star hotels. The total five star deluxe hotels have capacity of 12948 rooms and 55 five star hotel have capacity of 6654 rooms.

This table gives data about the hotels according to star. 1229 are the total available all type of hotels for with 68032 room accomadation.

Most of the projects on this illustrative list are not eligible for loans from the banks of the State Financial Agencies. It will be necessary to make suitable changes in the lending criteria for viable projects in the listed activities in order that their financial requirements are met.

The modification of the lending criteria of the State Financial agencies will be made with regard to the financial ceiling, debt equity ration, recovery period etc..

Necessary arrangements will be made to ensure that the state financial agencies and the banks attach adequate priority to the financial requirements of the tourism projects.

A new incentive package will be made available to replace the existing inventive policy instituted in 1991. A tax holiday of 5 - 10 years in respect of following taxes will be made available up to 100% of capital investment to various tourism projects located in special tourism areas whether declared by the Central Government on the state government located in designated areas and located on National and State highways. The scope and the extent of the benefits of tax holiday will vary according to certain considerations such as the admissible expenditure, the size of the capital investment etc.. The benefit of tax holiday will also be made available for the purpose of expansion of the existing tourism projects in these areas under

* Sales Tax
* Purchase Tax
* Electricity Tax
* Luxury Tax
* Entertainment Tax

Necessary administrative arrangement will be made at the State and District levels to implement the incentive schemes. Suitable scheme will be designed to market tourism products and particularly wide publicity will be secured in respect of various facilities being offered by the travel agents, tour operators etc. Special paying guest scheme will be formulated for providing adequate and inexpensive lodging and boarding facilities to take care of seasonal flows of tourists to the pilgrimage centers during festivals. Financial assistance will be provided for the preparation of feasibility reports by consultants in respect of tourism projects. Structure of the taxes and tariffs, e.g. luxury tax, entertainment tax, sales tax etc. will be received with reference to developmental needs of tourism sector and necessary amendments will be made .

Redefining the roles of the states and the markets

Since the approach of the Tourism Policy focuses on market led development, the role of the state would be as follows

• To ensure timely provision of necessary funding, the Government will earmark funds in the annual budgets of the departments concerned for securing the purpose mentioned.

• In conformity with state's promotional role in the development of tourism sector, all competitive and commercial activities of Tourism Corporation of Gujarat will be privatised except where no entrepreneur is coming forward to meet the existing need. This privatisation would help strengthen the financial position of the corporation and also help provide qualitative services to the tourists.

• Tourism corporation of Gujarat will assume a catalytic role focused on acting as clearing house of information, production and distribution of promotional literature, policy advice etc..

• The tourism corporation will assist entrepreneurs and agencies in tourism sector and will try to help alleviate their difficulties particularly vis a vis the Government and its agencies.

• A computerized information center will be set up at the state level to make available necessary information to the agencies / entrepreneurs who wish to set up tourism projects.

• In addition to its existing offices in Mumbai, Delhi and Chennai, the tourism corporation will also open its offices in other major cities of India to give wide publicity and disseminate information on Gujarat tourism and market tourism products through these offices and through reputed travel agents in other big cities. Thus, the information about Gujarat Tourism's tourist destinations and related information would be made available to tourists from outside the state in their own cities.

• There is already a scheme of 50% marketing grant from the state government to the local self governing bodies for the development of local tourists destinations. This scheme will be made more effective and attractive and necessary provisions in the budget will be made. This will help decentralize the process of developing tourist destinations.

• The process of decentralization will be further strengthened by delegation of administrative and executive power of approval of incentives to small tourism projects to district level bodies headed by the collector. These bodies, in addition will also secure co-ordination from other departments /

agencies of the Government in development and promotion of tourism representation will be given on this body to the experts, individual's agencies and individuals connected with the tourism.

- A single window clearance system will be instituted for speedy clearance of various permissions, approvals required under different laws and rules. Necessary modification / amendment will be made to various administrative arrangements and laws which are not consistent with the approach of this policy.   Care will be taken to ensure that prospective investors do not have to suffer from the complex administrative process.

- Intensive efforts will be undertaken to attract investors from outside the states as well as from other countries including non-resident Indians to invest in tourism sector large scale in Tourism corporation of Gujarat and Directorate of Tourism will play active role to ensure that investors get various permissions easily and are provided with all the necessary facilities.

- A high powered committee under the chairmanship of Chief Secretary with Director of Tourism as the member secretary will be constituted with the objective of securing effective co-ordination among various Government department and agencies as also to speed up decision making process concerning tourism. The committee will meet regularly and enjoy full powers of Government provided the approval of the Chief Minister and the council of minister will be obtained wherever required.

- In order to create a participative forum for deliberation and discussion concerning tourism industry, a tourism advisory council headed by the Chief Minister will be set up. The Ministers and Secretaries of administrative departments concerned will be the members. The representative of tourism industry, experts and related organizations will be nominated as members. The additional Chief Secretary (Tourism) will be the member of this council.

The council will meet periodically to deliberate upon policy as well as individual issues and offer suitable advice to the Government.

Perspective Planning

Perspective plan for tourism development will be prepared in consultation with experts. An overview of possible tourism products is offered below:

* ### *Pilgrimage and Archaeological Tourism*
    Gujarat has a preponderance of pilgrimage centers as in some other States. Somnath and Dwarka - some of the well known and revered sites of ancient Hindu temples are situated in the States. The temple architecture has reached heights of excellence in Jain temples at Shetrunji, Girnaar and Taranga. The temple of Ambaji situated in Aravalli range in North Gurajat is an important religious centre for devotes in the country. Dakor, Pavagadh, Bahucharaji, Shamalaji, Narayan Sarovar, Sudamals Porbandar, Kabirvad, Shuklatirth, Kayavarohan, Bhadrakali Temple- Ahmedabad and Maharshi Dayanand Sararwati's birth place are also important pilgrimage destinations which, have kept alive the religions of pilgrims visit these places every year.

    These places are visited not only by the devotees from all over the country but also by the non-resident Indians and travelers especially from the eastern part of the world. Necessary accommodation facilities and related service will be created on those sites. For ensuring orderly and planned development of Pilgrimage centres, the Government has constituted *"Pavitra Dhaam Vikas Board"* chaired by the Chief Minister. The Board will prepare and implement plans to provide necessary facilities to devotees and also ensure conservation of cultural atmosphere consistent with sentiments of visiting devotees.

    Shamalaji is an ancient site for Buddhists. The excavated relics of Buddhist period at the site are now kept in a museum of Baroda.

    There are number of places of archaeological importance such as the temple-town of Palitana, Modhera with its Sun Temple, historical Ranker Vav at Patan with relics of an ancient capital, the Girnar Hills with Hindu and Jain temples, Junagadh with a historical fort, Dabhoi, Champaner, Pavagadh, Shaking minarets, Gandhi Ashram, Siddi syed Jali etc. These can be developed by providing necessary infrastructural facilities and marketed as tourist destinations to attract tourists.

* ### Heritage Tourism
    A large number of old places, Havelis, Darbargadhs exist in the state. These historical building can be converted into hotels, restaurants or museums

by providing suitable incentives to owners. Wildlife and Pilgrimage Tourism Circuits can be linked to Heritage Properties exploiting the geographical congruity. Development of this subsector will not only attract foreigntourists but also provide encouragement and support to local art and craft.Government will take necessary steps to promote Heritage tourism in the state.

- **Wildlife Tourism**

There is a substantial scope for development of tourism based on wildlife in the state. Gir forest of Gujarat is the last stronghold of Asiatic Lions. The Bear Sanctuary at Ratan Mahal (Dist. Panch Mahal), Black Buck Sanctuary at Velgradar (Dist. Bhavnagar), Bird Sanctuary at Nal Sarovar (Dist. Ahmedabad), Wild Ass Sanctuary at Kutch etc. can be effectively developed into tourists destinations by providing infrastructural facilities. In order to facilitate visitors to these areas, coordination among various agencies will be established.

- **Coastal and Beach Tourism**

The Gujarat State has the longest coastline among maritime states of the country. Identified stretches of the coastline can be developed into beaches. From tourism point of view it will be the endeavor of state to develop beach potential by providing such facilities as may attract foreign tourists.
Various tourists destinations easily accessible from the coast will be linked through Coastal Shipping Circuits.

- **Tourism based on Traditional Arts, Crafts and Cultural Activities**

'Banni' in Kutch, Khambhat, Junagadh etc. are known for their craftmanship. Similarly there are hundreds of fairs that are celebrated through out the year with enthusiasm. Tarnetar fair in Surendranagar District, Chitra-Vichitra fair at Poshina in Sabarkantha District, Kanwat fair at Chhota Udepur District, Dang-Darbar in Dang, Bhavnath fair of Junagadh etc. have immense tourism value. By developing accommodation, transport and other facilities these fairs and festivals will be promoted nationally and internationally. The places of importance from art and craft point of view will be included in the tourist circuits and necessary facilities provided to tourists.

- **Co-operate Tourism**

Private sector will be encouraged to build the state of the art convention centres, seminar halls etc. so as to attract co-operative events like seminar, workshops and annual general meeting participant in such events generally have high purchasing power and provide a boost to local economy.

- **Adventure Tourism**

   This is also a territory with possibility of development as a sub-sector will be examined and new activities like Camel Safari in Kutch, Horse-Riding in Aravali Hill Ranges, Parachuting in Saputara, trekking in Dang, Pavagadh, Palitana etc. will be promoted. Such activities will create large scale employment opportunities for guides, coolies, traders for hire of tents and equipment etc. and will also encourage paying guest accommodation in such areas. Private entrepreneurs and institutions will be encouraged to develop such facilities.

- **Highway Tourism**

   There is good network of State and National Highways, which, criss-cross the state and large number of travelers prefer road journey. Because of large geographical expanse of the State, these journeys tend to be quite long and boring. There is a need for creating necessary facilities like hotels, restaurants, picnic spots, water parks etc. along the highways at suitable intervals for the highway travelers to relax. In fact, travelers can be induced to follow certain traffic routes if such facilities are better developed. Highway facilities and wayside amenities are so well developed in some states that this has become the mainstay of tourism. State shall encourage private investors to create such facilities on highways.

- Various sub-sectors of tourism activities listed above will be encouraged by marking new tourism units eligible for incentives under ' Tax Holiday ' incentive scheme in designated areas.

- As mentioned earlier, the State Government intends to designate certain areas having significant tourist potential as Special Tourism Areas. To his end, reputed consultants and institutions will be engaged to prepare area development plans in respect of various areas such as Kutch District areas around Sardar Sarovar project ares, South Saurashtra area covering Gir, Porbandar, Varaval, Somnath, Ahmedpur Mandvi etc. identified stretches of beaches and areas of pilgrimage / heritage towns. These areas will be developed by following interested area development approach. The State Government will make efforts to tap all the sources of national and international funding for development of these areas and provide special encouragement to tourism projects being established therein for ensuring faster development of these areas, Area Development Committee will be constituted.

Human Resource Development

Human Resource Development is an important aspect of service industries. Tourists depend upon travel agents, guides and hence trained manpower is a important for tourism industry. On the basis of available statistics, training facilities can be safely said to be totally inadequate if trained manpower is not available locally, the objective of local employment will not be achieved.

Keeping in view he approach of market-led development, the State Government will encourage and support certain of training facilities in the private sector by private agencies / individuals.

Hotel Management Courses, courses meant for guides, carter and other supervisory and non-supervisory staff of hotel will be introduced in industrial training institutes. Approved hotel associations and private entrepreneurs will be encouraged to create new training facilities making available land to them for this purpose and by giving other appropriate incentives. The Government will consider setting up a Hotel Management Training Institute at the state level preferably in private sector.

Residents of Gujarat, especially local youths would be encouraged and facilitated to take part in such training courses.

The institute of Hotel Management catering and nutrition which is working under the administrative control of the central Government will be utilized to start new training courses so that the residents of Gujarat can get admission and manpower requirement of this sector is met.

The residents of Gujarat undergoing such training will be reimbursement a part of the tuition fees through scholarship. To make the new tourism policy result oriented implementation will be monitored by a high powered committee under the chairmanship of chief secretary.

A management information system will be set up to assist the committee to make available information on various aspects of implementation on a continues basis the committee will also review the policy from time to time.

It's not one of India's most visited regions, but Gujarat was good enough for Krishna and Gandhi to hang out there, and has long been an important centre for Jains. Today, Gujarat is one of India's wealthiest states, supporting modern industrial complexes as well as thriving village handicrafts. The last

Asiatic lions are here, and the pleasant beaches are just perfect for plonking down with a scoop of wonderful Gujarati ice cream.

Gujarat has endured the longing gaze of many conquerors: Moghuls, Marathas, the Portuguese and the British have all rubbed their acquisitive hands while peering at the area's enticing perch on the Arabian Sea. Two hundred years of Muslim rule from the 13th century was initially marred by destructive impulses but later led to a fruitful amalgamation of Muslim, Jain and Hindu architecture, giving rise to the unique building styles still apparent in the area today. Surprisingly, the British were the least successful interlopers, the eastern portion of Gujarat surviving British rule as a collection of princely states right up to Independence. In 1960 the current borders of Gujarat were established, creating today's linguistically unified state.

Diu

One of India's undiscovered gems, Diu was a Portuguese colony until 1961 and the European influence is apparent in the wooden balconies, meandering and leafy lanes, and a couple of lonely churches. The tiny island of Diu is separated from the mainland by a narrow channel. Its crowning glory is the huge fort, a sight, which justifies the long trip here. The northern side of the island is tidal marsh and saltpans, while the southern coast alternates between limestone cliffs, rocky coves and the beaches where swimming is possible. The somewhat windswept and arid island is riddled with quarries from which the Portuguese removed vast quantities of limestone to construct their huge fort, city walls, monuments and buildings. Cheap and clean hotels are at a premium in Diu, but you might find a decent(ish) room around the town square. Buses run directly to the island from Veraval and Bhavnagar; otherwise, there are slow steam trains from Sasan Gir and Junagadh to Una, 10km from Diu.

Somnath

Along the coast to the west of Diu, Somnath is most famous for the long history and holiness of its temple, said to have been originally built out of gold by Somraj, the Moon God, later to be rebuilt by Rawana in silver, by Krishna in wood and then by Bhimdev in stone. None of this fazed Mahmud of Ghazni, an 11th-century Afghan king, drawn to this temple so wealthy that it had 300 musicians, 500 dancing girls and even 300 barbers to shave the heads of visiting pilgrims. Mahmud took the town, moved on to the temple, looted it, then destroyed it just to show he really meant business. So began a pattern of Muslim destruction and Hindu rebuilding which continued for centuries. The builders gave up for a couple of hundred years until 1950 when the current monastery spewed forth from the ruins. To the east of the town is the confluence of three rivers where Lord Krishna was mistaken for a deer (easy to do). There are plenty of buses running from Junagadh and Veraval and there is a vast guesthouse near the temple.

The last home of the Asiatic lion is 100km north-west of Diu. The sanctuary, which covers 1400 sq km, has proved a haven for the growlers who are breeding keenly: there are now about 300 lions roaming around, up from under 200 in 1980.

Apart from the lions there are also bears, hyenas, foxes, deer and antelope, including the graceful chinkara gazelle and the canine-oriented barking deer. Peacocks preening and monkeys doing the monkey thang can also be seen on safaris. The best time to visit the sanctuary is from December to April, and it is closed completely from mid-May to mid-October. There are a couple of lodges at Sasan Gir village (where you can pick up a safari permit and a guide), and buses travel frequently between the sanctuary and Junagadh, 50km to the north.

Bhuj

Bhuj is an old walled city in the Kutch region. Kutch, in western Gujarat, is virtually an island; indeed, during the monsoon period from May onwards, it really is an island. Bhuj resembles the state of much of India before the tourist invasion. People remain largely unaffected by what goes on outside the area, so you're much more likely to come across the disarming hospitality which was once the hallmark of rural India. Where else would someone offer you a lift on their bicycle? You can lose yourself for hours in the maze-like streets and alleyways of this town. There are walls within walls, crenellated gateways, old palaces with intricately carved wooden pavilions, Hindu temples decorated with the gaudy, gay abandon of which only tribal people seem capable, equally colourful tribespeople, and camels pulling huge cartfuls of produce into the various markets. The villages of the Kutch region are also worth exploring as each specialises in a different form of handicraft, from block-printing to nut-cutting. There are pleasant guesthouses in the heart of the bazaar. Trains connect daily to Ahmedabad and a quicker service runs overnight through Gandhidham

Palitana

Just over 50km south-west of Bhavnagar, Palitana is the gateway to one of Jainism's holiest pilgrimage places. Over a period of 900 years, 863 temples have been built on the hilltop overlooking the town, and even after large-scale Muslim campaigns of destruction in the 14th and 15th centuries, the crest looks like a giant, glistening marble wedding cake. The most notable of the temples is dedicated to Shri Adishwara, the first *tirthankar* (Jain prophet or 'Finder of the Path'). Adjacent is the Muslim shrine of Angar Pir. Women who want to have children make offerings of miniature cradles at this shrine. Buses connect daily with Diu and Ahmedabad, and there are some good hostels in the centre of town.

Junagadh

Few travellers make the trip out to Junagadh, but it's an interesting town right at the base of the temple-studded Girnar Hill. The city dates from 250 BC and is full of exotic old buildings, most in a state of disrepair. As well as the gargantuan fort, the temples, mosques and the intricate mausoleum, the soft rock on which Junagadh is built encouraged the construction of caves and wells. Some ancient Buddhist caves cut in the hillside to the east of the city are thought to be at least 1500 years old.

The 600m climb up 10,000 stone steps to the Jain temples on the summit of Girnar is best made at dawn. (That way you have the rest of the day to recover). You'll see monkeys by the path and eagles soaring overhead, and you'll wonder why the monkeys are laughing at your red face and why the eagles got all the wings. If you really can't face the walk, *doolies* (rope chairs) carried by porters can be hired; for these you pay by weight, so you have to suffer being weighed on a huge beam scale, just like a sack of grain. However, given that taking your belly to India is now a recognised supermodel diet strategy the indignity may not be too great. There are regular bus and train connections to Ahmedabad and Mumbai (Bombay), as well as the Sasan Gir Lion Sanctuary, 50km south.

Junagarh has a museum is set in the Sakkarbagh complex, with a fine collection of prehistoric stone and bone implements, sculptures, manuscripts, copper inscriptions, handicrafts and princely relics dating to the reign of the Nawab including porcelain, glassware, carpets and silver. More relics of the nawab can be seen at the Darbarhall museum which is housed in a former palace, with its silver polished throne, howdahs and palanquins, gem studded carpets, arm and armour, paintings, photographs and portraits.

Further north of Junagdh, Rajkot has one of Saurtshtra's most attractive museums, the Watson museum, named for colonel Watson who was the local political agent from 1886 to 1893. The museum has a Durbar displaying royal portraits of the princes of Saurashtra, portraits of royals and European guests, Albert Gilbert's sculptural reproduction of Queen Victoria dated to 1899, archaeological finds from different periods, medieval manuscripts and miniatures, historic inscriptions, prehistoric exhibits, fine bronzes and other historic displays. The first floor mainly dedicated to ethnology offering an insight into the culture of Rabaris, Ahirs and Mehrs, handicrafts, musical instruments and utensils of Saurashtra.

Jamnagar

Jamnagar is a sizeable city way off the tourist trail. It's best known today for the Bala Hanuman Temple where, since 1964, there's been 24-hour continuous chanting of the temple becomes lively and animated when people come to promenade, and *chai* and *kulfi* stalls set up and ply their trade. There are heaps of cheap hotels in Jamnagar, with the dosshouses near the railway station winning our prize for most disgusting in India. The hotels in the centre of town are a better bet. There are direct trains from Jamnagar to Ahmedabad, Mumbai (Bombay) and **Dwarka.**

Gandhiji was born at Porbandar in 1869 AD. His father, Karamchand Gandhi, was the minister of the royal family of Porbandar, and his home was a mansion near the Darbargadh palace complex. Just next to Gandhiji's home is the Kirti mandir commissioned to commemorate the birthplace of the world's best loved Gujarati. Gandhiji went to school at Rajkot, where his childhood home is now a memorial. A plaque outside the Shamaldas Arts College and Sir P P Science Institute campus reminds students that Gandhiji was a alumni of this 1885 AD university, and the Gandhi Smriti in the Barton museum building has copies of his mark sheets. After spending some time overseas, Gandhiji returned to India and soon after that established his Kochrab ashram at Ahmedabad, from where he moved to a new site on the banks of the river Sabarmati in 1917 AD. The Sabarmati ashram was the launching pad of Gandhiji's many movements including the struggle for freedom from British rule, the fight against caste discrimination in India, and the swadeshi movement. The Hriday kunj where he stayed houses his simple belongings, while Charles Correa has designed a suitable memorial keeping in mind Gandhiji's policy of simplicity and non- possession. In 1921 Gandhiji inaugurated the Gujarat Vidyapith which is working on tribal welfare research even today.

Gandhi ashram was the staging post for Gandhiji's march to Dandi in 1930 AD. The march protesting against the salt act, that prevented Indians from earning from salt trade, ended at Dandi with the Mahatma picking salt from the coastal marshes, an act that broke the back of the British empire in India by inspiring various patriotic uprisings. A memorial and a picture gallery marks the spot where Gandhiji's disobedience act was committed. Gandhiji left Gujarat after the Dandi march and settled in Mumbai, Dehii and other cities of India, but the Satyagraha, self government and village upgradation movements he had instilled with the help of Sardar Patel, starting with south Gujarat, remained alive after his death. In 1942, Ahmedabad was one of the focal points for the Quit India movement. Gujarat has many Gandhian institutions and ashrams based on his principles today.

In Marketing Management the 4 P,s viz; Price , Promotion, Place and Product are the important factors. These factors are very important in the marketing of tourism which is essentially a service industry. Study and analysis of the topic under investigation has been done from the point of view the 4 P's mentioned above.

The history of Gujarat that can be measured by time dates hack to the last stages of the fourth century B.C. The history of human culture prior to that period begins with the Stone Age. The references of Gujarat and Saurashtra are to be found in the Mahabharat, 'Arthashastra' of Chanakya, Deval Smriti and Buddha stories written during the 1st century A.D. Clear references to Saurashtra in the stone inscriptions at Girnar, of Maha Kshatrap Rudradama of 15O A.D, of the remains and reminiscences of the people living at Rozdi (Shrinathgadh) near Gondal in Saurashtra of 1850 B.C. and different strata of cultural life found at various places prove that the culture of Gujarat is at least no less than 4,000 years old !

According to the Hindu epics, Lord Krishna and his elder brother Balarama, evacuated Mathura and established themselves at Kushasthali, now known as Dwarka and started what is known as the Yadava dynasty. Dwarka subsequently became one of the four seats (mathas) set up by Adi Shankaracharya.

The Parsees when they fled from Iran in the eighth century first landed at Sanjan on the shores of Gujarat with the holy flame, which still burns in Udwada in Valsad. The Muslim influence left its lasting imprints on the local art and architecture and it came to be known as the Indo-Saracenic style.

Among the earliest Europeans in Gujarat were the Portuguese who settled in Diu, a small island off the southern coast of Saurashtra. After that came the British who set up warehouses in Surat in 1612.

Gujarat was a part of the erstwhile Mumbai state during the British Rule. But in 1960, the 'Gujarati' population decided to secede from that union, which resulted in the formation of two new states, namely Gujarat and Maharashtra. The new State of Gujarat came into existence on 1st May, 1960 because of this bifurcation.

Gujarat is the birthplace of many who played an important role in shaping modern India. Prominent among them are Shri Dadabhoy Navroji, the grand old man of the freedom fight, Sardar Vallabhbhai Patel, the architect of a united India and Mahatma Gandhi, the father of the Nation. These men carried the torch of national freedom and integration infusing the qualities of tolerance, brotherhood, non-violence and patriotism amongst Indians.

Gujarat gets its name from "Gujjar Rashtra", the land of the Gujjars, a migrant tribe who came to India in the wake of the invading Huns in the 5th century. The history of Gujarat dates back to 2000 BC. It is also believed that Lord Krishna left Mathura to settle on the west coast of Saurashtra at Dwarka.

The state saw various kingdoms like Mauryas, Guptas, Pratiharas etc, but it was under the regime of Chalukyas (Solanki) Gujarat witnesses progress and prosperity. Inspite of the plundering of Mahmud of Ghazni, the Chalukyan kings were able to maintain general prosperity and well being of the state. After this glorious respite, Gujarat faced troubled times under the Muslims, Marathas and the British rules.

The dark ages ruled after the death of lord Krishna and no accurate information has been made available about the huge leap of 3000 years till we reach Ashoka, the great. 3000 years slide away into oblivion and we come to the Emperor Ashoka, whose tales tell the stone inscriptions at the foot of Girnar. Chandragupta Maurya had a sovereign rule from Patliputra in Magadha in 319 B.C. Saurashtra and Gujarat were also part of his expanding Kingdom. The autonomy of the Kings Bindusaar and Ashoka remained a glorious facet of the Maurya rule.

Ashoka was a war loving king and his main ambition in life was to capture as many territories and kingdoms as possible. Cruelty, treachery and violence of battles, on his way to Kalinga, however, aroused in him the fear of God and the love of human beings. This divine transformation gave him the title of Priyadarshi. Ashoka had several stuti stambhs, singing the praises of God and establishing sermons and religious dictums for the reformation of the people and for reinstating the faith of his subjects. The stone inscriptions at the foothills of Girnar, preach the eternal message of non-violence, peace and love towards human beings as propagated by Lord Buddha. The seal of that pillar, has been sacred for Indians for centuries and now presides over our conscious patriotism in the form of our National Emblem - The Ashoka Chakra.

The poet Nanhalal had described the 4m tall and 8m round stone at Girnar as 'Shailakan' (the molecule of a stone) in his famous poem 'At the foot of Girnar' (Girnar ne charne).

The inscriptions sing praises of three great Indian emperors : Ashoka, Kshatrap and Skadagupta. These monarchs ruled between 234-237 B.C., 150 A.D. and 456 A.D. respectively. The inscriptions of Ashoka are in the Prakrit language and the rest are in Sanskrit. The Brahmi script, the mother of Devnagari, Gujarati, Bengali, Telugu and Tamil scripts was used during those times.

The Present state of Gujarat was formed in 1st May 1960, as a result of Bombay Reorganization act, 1960. The state is bounded by the Arabian Sea on the west, Pakistan and Rajasthan in the north and north-east respectively, Madhya Pradesh in the south east and Maharashtra in south. **3.8 Milestones**

* 2500 BC. Harappans appeared from Northern India to settle down, and established over a hundred towns and cities.

* 100 to 500 BC. Yadavas, Krishna's clan, held power over much of Gujarat, with their capital at Dwarka.

* 200 BC. Political history began with the powerful Mauryan empire, established by Chandragupta with its capital at Junagadh, and reached its peak under Ashoka.

* 100 AD. Satraps, members of the Saka tribes, gained control over Saurashtra.

* 388 AD. Guptas, and then Maitrakas, established their their capital at Valabhi.

* 1100 AD. Saurashtra came under sway of the Solanki (Chauhan) dynasty.

* 1299 AD. Khalji conquested and the Muslim rule was established.

*   1307 AD. Muzaffar Shah's declaration of independence from Delhi marked the foundation of the Sultanate of Gujarat.

*   1500 AD. Moghul emperor Akbar conquested.

*   1531 AD. The Portuguese, already settled in Goa, captured Daman and Diu.

*   1613 AD. The British East India Company set up original Indian headquarters in Surat.

*   1818 AD. British sovereignty was established.

*   1960 AD. Bombay state was split and Gujarat state was created.

*   Today. Gujarat's textile industry is still the largest in India, with the trading of the business-minded community helping to maintain its wealth

The people and their habitat

The State of Gujarat is inhabited by many people of different ethnic origins, belonging to different social communities and following different religious beliefs. The variety of groups, which are distinct from one another in their language and social and cultural traditions resulted from successive immigrations from land as well as from the sea. While the Aryans came by land, the Persians, the Arabs and the

Africans came by sea, but irrespective of their route of immigration, they were fused into a mass of humanity which carries groups of people with distinct physical and cultural traits. The Aryans were perhaps the first people to come from the north, who either conquered or drove away the Bhils, the traditional rulers of Gujarat. Apart from these two distinct classes, the Aryans now commonly recognized as Hindus and the Bhils, a third class of people known as 'Kolis' are equally important and occupy an intermediate social position between the Aryans and the Bhils. The immigration during the medieval period brought Islam and Zoroastrianism to Gujarat and initiated the growth of a multi-religious society. Subsequent developments and the internal migrations in the country led to the growth of a society in Gujarat which is characterized by the following religions and regional groups:

Religious groups
* Hindus
* Buddhists
* Jains

* Muslims
* Christians
* Aboriginals **Hindus**

Vedic Dharma was popular and from the remains found from the Indus valley Civilization, it is believed that worship of goddesses, Sun, Shiva, was followed. The temple of Somnath, in western coast, is one of the twelve jyotirllingas of Shiva. There is no definite records of the origin of the temple (which is believed to have been built during Mahabharat times) but the earliest record is of the dates of 10th century. In northern Gujarat, there is an eleventh-century Sun-Temple, at Modhera.

Near Mehsana, the town of Siddhpur is known for Rudramala Temple,built in 12th century. Gooddess-worship was followed in ancient times and popular amongst them are temples at Pavagarh,

Kherhbrahma and Ambaji. The oldest temple of Dwarika has become a pilgrimage place to worship Krishna.

Jains

The Jainism is widely followed in Gujarat since years. The oldest temple is believed to be of Shankheshwar Parshwanath in North Gujarat. Taranga temples were built during the Solanki period and they are better preserved than the temples of Mount Abu, Girnar and Shatrunjay. Palitana, is India's principal Jain pilgrimage site, the temples dated 5th century.

Muslims

Through the sea-route which was open for trade, the people from Iran and Arabic countries started coming in Gujarat. The trade system was established and the Indo-Islamic culture got flourished. This is a marked feature of many Gujarati cities. The famous mosques are built during Mughul times. These include Sidi

Sayyid's mosque, Jami Masjid, of Ahmedabad,, Alif Khan's mosque in Dholka, Jama Masjid of Bharuch,etc.

Buddhists

About the same time as Jainism, Buddhism also got popular. There were Buddhist temples also and the remains of the same are found from all over

Gujarat. Ashokan Buddhist edicts engraved on a rock are near Junagadh. These remains are of 3rd century BC.

Parsis

In 10th century, Iranian Jarthost followers came to Gujarat and got settled here first at Diu, and then at Sanjan, Udvada -in South of Gujarat. Sanjan and Udvada are today main pilgrimage places of Parsi followers.

Regional groups

- Kutchis
- Kathis
- Aboriginals

Gujaratis, a most comprehensive group covering the entire population of the state

Despite the fact that the peninsula of Kathiawar is named after the Kathis, the latter are no longer the only people in Saurashtra. Successive waves of immigrants from other parts of India have led t the superimposition of different communities and cultures Kathiawar. The powerful royal families, which conquered Saurashtra later on, established their rule, letting the Kathis accept their sovereignty and follow their own pastoral occupations or take to more settled occupations like farming.

The nomadic people of Kathiawar without past royal glory like that of Kathis are the ' Rabaris They are essentially a community of cattle-breeders who have migrated from Sindh and Marwar and claim a Rajput ancestry. Tall, strong and well-built, the Rabaris stand out prominently by their features and dress. Often they lead a nomadic life.

The Gujaratis, the people of Gujarat, are found all over the State. These people trace their lineage from the people originally known as Gurjars, after whom Gujarat is named. They are believed to have come to India with Huns and passing through Punjab settled in Gujarat. Gujaratis were highly influenced by the cultural waves from the mainland and accepted the monarchies that ruled over them. Various Hindu traditions like Shaivism and Vaishnavism which sprang upon the mainland were imbibed by Gujarat which in turn developed its own galaxy of saints and devotees and its own art and culture. The successive waves of immigration were absorbed in the society that was fast evolving and today the word Gujarati does not seem to suggest any definite association with a particular stock, a tribe of immigrants, or a specific group of people.

Though the general term 'Gujaratis' can be applied to the entire population of the State of Gujarat, the sense of regional affiliation, which in certain cases reflects a common origin, is so strong that a feeling of group identification of common interests is developed and which the members of groups are reluctant to part with. The Kutchis, the natives of peninsula of Kutch, a district of Gujarat, have their own dialects, and while letting themselves be known as ' Gujaratis,' outside the State, they prefer to retain their identity as a people within the State.

The Kutchis are both Hindus and Muslims and a large number of them have migrated from Sindh. the Jadeja Rajputs, the Lohanas, and even the Muslims many of whom are Maldharis, the cattle-breeders, have all come from Sindh consequent upon their defeat at the hands of some kings or as a result of some religious persecution.

Unlike the Kutchis, the Kathis, the settlers of Kathiawar, after whom the peninsula was named, came to Saurashtra at the close of the fourteenth century. Their origin is not fully known but it is quite possible that they were driven southwards by the Muslim invaders. Khachar and Chotila were the most important seats of the Kathis. Worshippers of sun, they were essentially nomadic and had, among other pastoral occupations, developed the art of hours-breeding.

The castes and sub-castes among the Hindus of Gujarat are strictly adhered to. Besides the ' Brahmins ' and the ' Banias ' whose functions and occupations are fairly well determined, the community of ' Patidars ' owning land is the strongest force in the economic and political life of the State. Patidars, also called Patels, are the best agriculturists of Gujarat. Often they have a share in the village in which they live. They are grouped into four categories - Levas, Kadawas, Anjana and Uda. Of these, the Levas are concentrated in central Gujarat, whereas the Kadawas are most numerous in Mehasana district.

The fourth regional group which may have been a native of Gujarat, but which does not resemble any of the previous groups, is the community of aboriginals living in the rugged borderlands of the State. The aboriginals, locally known as 'Bhils', inhabit the hilly tracts of Gujarat that border the plains from Abu in the north to Dangs in the south. The Bhils may be regarded as a hybrid group in Gujarat, on the one hand absorbing Rajput blood and on the other representing a tribal sub-stratum. Some believe that the Bhils are the Aryans of the outer band in Gujarat. They were driven from the plains into the adjacent hills by the next major Aryan wave which belonged to the inner band. According to their own oral tradition, the Bhils regard themselves as belonging to the Kshatriya caste who had to take shelter in the hills of the Vindhyas and the Satpuras along the lower Narmada to save themselves from the wrath of the Brahmin hero, Parashuram. The Bhils of Gujarat thus do not possess any racial basis distinct from the other inhabitants of the region.

The tribals of Gujarat are found concentrated in the south-eastern part of Gujarat particularly in the districts of Panchmahals, Surat, Baroda and Broach, of which the first two have the maximum number. The majority of the total tribal population is composed of Bhils. The main tribal groups are the Bhils, the Dublas, the Naika-Narkdas, the Gamits and the Dhankas. The infertile soil in the hilly areas of tribal settlements has left no choice except that of subsistence farming to the tribal people. Rice, jowar, bajri and gourndnut are the main crops grown by them. For three or four months in the year, these tribals engage themselves in wood-cutting with which they descend to the small towns for getting the daily necessaries of life. Many have been engaged in organized forest industry, some collect lac and toddy but the general economic level of their society is still very low. Tied down to their own where they are governed by their own social laws, the tribals of Gujarat have yet to develop an awareness of the fast-changing social and economic condition of life in the out world.

The Villages in Gujarat

A village is an expression of community living with agriculture as its essential base. As an important element in the rural landscape, the villages occupy the valleys, the alluvial interfluves or any other site that ensures some economic return from the soil or offers opportunities for sedentary occupations like fishing. In the plains of Gujarat susceptible to periodic inundation, a village occupies a site above flood level and very often on the fertile alluvial terraces. But in Saurashtra, the villages are often on the banks of a stream which, while assuring perennial supply of underground water from the wells in its bed, does not bring on devastating floods so very common in the Narmada and the Tapi. Most of the villages in the Gujarat plains and even in Saurashtra are accessible by automobile during the dry part of the year, and they are usually located on an approach road branching off from the main road. The villages along the main roads are invariably large and have developed a large segment of non-agricultural occupation. Accessibility to these villages is considerably reduced during the monsoons when water-logging in the coastal areas and small flooded streams in the plains make the movement of vehicular traffic difficult. Irrespective of seasons, the hilly villages are always less accessible, since transport is not well developed in these areas.

The built-up area of an average village is a mass of unplanned houses with mud walls and tiled roofs. An exception has to be made here in the case of the villages of Charotar which are large and, with more than 50% of their houses built of brick and stone, resemble a small town. In all the villages, however, the lanes are narrow and circuitous in which the effluent from the houses on each side is discharged. Sometimes a house is occupied by several families in which case the rooms or blocks are allocated to individual families. This often results from the breaking-up of the joint family and partition among its members.

The general lay-out of the village and its morphology, however vary widely from one region to another. In south Gujarat, a village is a cluster of houses with no definite plan and often interested by a street and a few lanes. The house frontages are not in a straight line and their facades have no uniformity. The village is arbitrarily divided into 'mohollas', named after a community or an important ancestor. The roofs of the houses are invariably sloping and are tiled, thatched or covered with corrugated iron sheets. Wood is used extensively as a building material, and elaborate carving on the threshold is a common features of the houses belonging to the head of the village or a prosperous farmer. The interior is decorated with a series of utensils of all sizes displayed on shelves panelled against the walls. In the more prosperous region of central Gujarat, the village is characterized by rows of houses, each row inhabited by a particular community. In the centre of the village is the Panchayat office and a "chora", a miniature square. Many of these villages are electrified and have a dispensary, a primary school and a high school, besides a temple, a mosque, a burning-ghat and a graveyard. Often one finds the village gods installed on all corners of a village. Communal grouping of houses is very apparent. Some of the local communities named after their professions like Thakarda, Patidar, Wankar, Suthar and Chambadia occupy rows of blocks in strips. Thus there often emerge parallel strips, each inhabited largely by a single community. Big villages in central Gujarat have a variety of residential structures. A flat-roofed house built of bricks and cement is symbolic of one's prestige and is often built by big cultivators, usually the Patels. The houses with mud walls and tiled and thatched roofs belong to the poorer sections of the population like Bharwads, the cattle-breeders. The low rainfall of the area has done away with the necessity of solid houses with sloping roofs that have to stand stormy monsoons. The houses belonging to the lower economic group appear fragile but are well kept.

A village in Saurashtra presents a different spectacle. Its lay-out is different from a village in central Gujarat. Often the villages are on the river-side. The importance of the latter can be assessed by the existence of several wells in the bed of rivers themselves. In areas of low rainfall, the basaltic rocks with their partial impermeability present a serious problem of water supply and the villages are drawn close to the rivers. The systematic rows of houses typical of central Gujarat villages tend to assume a pattern in Saurashtra which suggests greater individual independence. The orientation of the settlement is often linear, spreading along the river and divided by a lane often running parallel to the river. This compact and linear pattern of the village usually along the river-side changes into a village of scattered houses bearing hardly any relation with the rivers in the alluvial parts of the coastal districts. The temple, the school and the 'chora' remain, however, the common features of a village in all parts of Saurashtra. The village tank so typical of south and south-central Gujarat is also found in Saurashtra, but is not common in the river-side villages.

The house type remains essentially the same in all parts of Saurashtra and the variations show only the economic status of the households. Middle-class houses, the largest in number, do not have an enclosed courtyard and could be described as a rectangular block divided into one or two rooms on the rear and a verandah in the front, a part of which is sometimes used as a kitchen. The building material is the uncut basalt piled up with clay as mortar to form the walls, which support the sloping tiled roofs. The richer villagers build 'pucca' houses, flat-roofed and well-ventilated. Such houses are, however, rare.

The settlement and life of a Saurashtra village is often dominated by 'Kolis', 'Kathis' and 'Rabaris'. These communities, though not on the same social and economic level as the 'Thakardas' and 'Patidars' of central Gujarat, play an equally important role in the village life of Saurashtra. While the Kathis are prosperous and own lands, the Kolis are often landless labourers and are sometimes engaged in skilled arts like stone-cutting. The Rabaris, on the other hand, are cattle-breeders with a nomadic habit which is fast disappearing. This perhaps is one of the reasons why a Rabari village in Saurashtra is not a compact unit and appears like a random grouping of temporary huts. Other, communities which inhabit the villages of Saurashtra include 'Bharwad', 'Lohana' and artisans like tailors, potters, carpenters and barbers.

A village in north Gujarat is not very different from the one in central Gujarat and Saurashtra. Occuring in a semi-arid region, the villages rely for their supply of water on tanks lying on their outskirts. A temple on one side and a deep well inside are occasionally associated with the tank. A well inside the tank is fairly common all over Gujarat and is possibly a way out to save part of the tank from pollution by enclosing it in a well which is perennial in normal years, in contrast to other wells which run dry during summer. Communal segregation is common in a village and one does find groups of houses belonging to Patidars, 'Prajapatis' and Thakardas.

The houses occur in rows, often with common outer walls, with the result that no space is left between them. These are made of stone, brick or mud and could have a flat roof as in the case of a well-built house of a Patidar, or a sloping roof covered with tiles. In some cases, however, the roof could be even a thatched canopy on a circular hut. These three types represent the three economic classes in village. The houses have generally poor ventilation, low roofs and appears more like temporary shelters. An open varandah in front of the house is common and appears indispansable in view of the climatic conditions of the area and the social requirements of the family characterised by an exclusive get-together of males in the evenings.

Physiography

The state of Gujarat occupies northern extremity of the western sea-board of India. It comprises three geographical regions.

- The peninsula, traditionally known as Saurashtra. It is essentially a hilly track sprinkled with low mountains.
- Kutch on the north --east is barren and rocky and contains the famous Rann (desert) of Kutch, the big Rann in the north and little Rann in the east.
- The mainland extending from the Rann of Kutch and Aravalli Hills to the river Damanganga is on the whole a level plain of alluvial soil.

The Rivers

The plains of Gujarat are watered by rivers like
- Sabarmati
- Mahi

- Narmada
- Tapi
- Banad
- Saraswati
- Damanganga

Rainfall

The rainfall in the state, except in the arid zones of Surendranagar and north Gujarat, varies between 65 and 127 cms.

Climate

As the Tropic of Cancer passes though the northern border of Gujarat, the State has an intensely hot or cold climate. But the Arabian sea and the Gulf of Cambay in the west and the forest-covered hills in the east soften the rigorous of climatic extremes.

Agriculture

Some of the features regarding agriculture are listed below :

- Gujarat ranks first in the country in the production of cotton and groundnut.
- Gujarat ranks second in the country in the production of cotton and tobacco.
- Other important cash crops are *isabgol, cumin, sugarcane, mangoes and bananas.*
- The chief food crops of the state are *paddy, wheat and bajra. Tuwar* and maze are produced in local areas.
- Valsad has become India's first integrated hoticulture district - which is expected to boost exports of vegetables, fruits and flowers from the country.
- Gujarat has 19.66 lakh hectares of land under forest. Forest spices available in the state are teak, *khair, sadad and manual bamboos.*

Industry

Recently, Gujarat has experienced a rapid industrial growth and has become one of the important industrialized States of the country. Some the features regarding its industries are listed below :

- Gujarat has a dominant electronic industry.
- New industries, which are coming up, are chemicals, petrochemicals, fertilizer, drugs, and pharmaceuticals, dye-stuffs and engineering units of multiple types.
- In 1990-91 Gujarat ranked second after Maharashtra (22.7 in percentage share in gross value of output).
- The state is major producer of inorganic chemicals such as Soda-ash and Caustic soda as well as chemical fertilizers.
- It has the largest petro-chemical complex in the country.
- The dairy industry has made tremendous advancement and the state accounts for nearly 63 per cent of infant milk produced in the country. In milk procurement, Gujarat (35 lakh litres) is first in India, followed by Maharashtra (21.5 lakh), Tamil Nadu (15 Lakh) and Karnataka (14 Lakh).
- Fish production 1994-95 was 7 lakh tonnes worth Rs. 852 crore.
- Exploration and production of oil refinery at Koyali are other industrial achievement.
- Near Bharuch Gujarat Narmada Valley Fertilizer Company has achieved great success.
- Ankleshwar Industrial estate is humming with a number of industries.
- On the coastal areas of Saurashtra ship-breaking yards have taken shape at Alang and Sachana.
- Jamnagar, Porbandar, Jaftabad, Bhavnagar etc. are busy with new industries, trade and business.
- The number of registered working factories were 20050 at the end of year 2000 with the average daily employment of 8.68 lakh.
- The number of small scale industrial units was 2,56,388 as on March 31, 2003.
- Gujarat is major salt producing state and its production forms as much as 60 per cent of the country's output.
- Gujarat is endowed with one major port Kandla, 11 intermediate ports and 29 minor ports dotting its coastal boundary.
- Gujarat has the first position in national project on Biogas (28000 plants in 94-95).

- The first expressway of the nation is in Gujarat between Ahmedabad and Vadodara.
- An I.T. city at Gandhinagar and a software tower at Ahmadabad are planned.

Roads

The total length of roads - 73,397 km are (1999-2000) . The first expressway of the nation is in Gujarat between Ahmedabad and Vadodara.

Table

Types and Distance of Road.

Types of Road	Distant in (k.m)
National Highway Road	1570
State Highway Road	19761
Main Dist. Road	20815
Other Dist.Road	10435
Village Road	19584
Total	72165

(Source) General Administration Information book Gujarat state Gandhinagar

Culture

Gujarat possesses natural beauty in great bounty. The East is covered by Sahyadri and Satpuda mountain range. In the West is the desert of Kachchha and Arabian Sea (Ratnakar Sagar). In the North are the hills of Mount Abu and Aravalli and in the South the river Daman Ganga flows through all the times. Amid this glory, the ocean abounding in folk culture has rhythmic cadence and gentle breezes in the life of its people and that is its ethos.

Man : The creator of Culture

The word folk culture consists of two words. 'Folk' and 'culture'. 'Folk' and 'of the folk' - 'pertaining to the folk' -being used in expression since Vedic times. That which does not relate to Vedas has been termed 'of the folk' - 'pertaining of folk'. In this word 'folk culture', 'folk' means a group of people (not small) engaged in agriculture and agri-based occupations and live amidst the age old traditions, amid the under-currents of everflowing tradition, that includes rustic living in rural areas as well as forest dwellers of hilly areas.

Folk culture could be considered as the psychological expression of ADIMANAV, the oldest lot of human beings on earth. The concept of religion prevalent among the folk, their trust, faith, even blind faith, conservatism, old traditions, customs and rituals, unwritten literature-that dwelt on tongue and being recited-fancy and fantasy of ghosts and witches, hypnotic, Tavij, deities and divinities, dresses and costumes, dialects, festivals, celebrations, brawls, scuffles, duels, combats and battles, arms and weapons, animal husbandry, navigation, tillage-whatever mentally and physically was available to the soul of the folk-all this is enshrined in the ambit of folk culture. Folk culture is the creation of the folk mass. It is the collective outcome. People for the sake of their conveniences, facilities and liking, began with some rite-rituals, customs and continued traditions which subsequently happen to be the main aspects and ingredients of folk life. Thus, literature, arts, creative activity and religion - the main and supportive pillars of folk culture are the creations of human endeavor and not the outcome of Nature and godly efforts. Therefore, it could be said that folk culture is as old or ancient as the human race on earth.

Folk-culture of Gujarat must have its origin on the banks of river Sabarmati where men of old living in kubas (round shape huts) prepared by them might also have created its cradle. Whereas folk culture of Saurashtra (sorath-saurashtra) had its cradle in nesda wherein forest dwellers engaged in animal husbandry must be its original craftsmen.

Research by Dr. Sankalia on the Sabarmati Valley Civilization supports this fact that before the development of Mohenjo-Dero and Harappan civilization of Urbanity, folk civilization of nomadic tribes was in existence. Reminiscences of that of animals, plants, trees, and of the deities-gods and goddesses and even in the worship of or faith in BHUVA necromancers and removers of ills and evils through magic, strange recitation of mantras and performance of irrational rituals.

Since ancient times, human beings had started living in lush green forests and hills, on the banks of rapidly flowing rivers and on the wide and vast coasts of the seas. The people of Gujarat are endowed in their living and culture with varied aspects and elemental simplicities of that very Nature which has given them love of nature, simple pleasures, love for truth, non-sophistication and straight-forwardness, being the dominant factors shaping their lives and culture. From the deep and narrow valleys of high dyked hills, streaming and flowing rivers have nourished in the life of the folk, virtues of valor, bravery and chivalry coupled with love and loyalty.

On account of human beings settled in this pleasant soil of Gujarat with a coast of sea of about 1600 km to its West, since ancient times, the shaping spirit of its culture is naturally the endless sea and maritime climate. About eight thousand years ago, a tribe called nishad living the life of fishermen put their first steps on the land of gujarat. koli, kharva, vagher, and miyana of the present are considered as successors to nishad tribe. in fifth century B.C. came to Gujarat lonians, Beks, Yons and Greek tribes and brought with them wooden deities and worship of Gods and Goddesses. Reminiscences of Greek culture relating to this are still found extant in MER community of BARDA hills. About five thousand years ago from amongst the wandering tribes that came to Gujarat, Gop culture emerged. yadava and ahira coming from mathura and brindavan brought with them raaslila (art of dancing with singing, using flutes and wooden sticks). their daughter-in-laws taught lasya nritya to the gopis of dwarka. dandiya raas of today in its origin is the gift of that tribe and this gop culture subsequently gave birth to several unique festivals in gujarat. it also generated fairs (mela) giving joy and rapture to human hearts both of males and females. During Tenth century, came to Saurashtra white hun (mongols) who brought here sun worship. this hun of yore are the kathi darbars of our time. horse, she-buffalo and weapons are the main ingredients of their culture.

Numerous sea-faring tribes came to the seacoast of Saurashtra. Anthropologists believe that most of the tribes that settled in Gujarat, have come from other regions of the country and the continent. From North came Aryans, Rajputs and Gurjars. From South Kanbis, Siddis and Arabs (therefore Ratnakar Sagar bears the name of Arabian Sea) came through sea routes.

Baluchs and Lohanas came traversing the desert of Kachchha. Subsequently from time to time with the passing of years came more than one hundred and seventy tribes in Kathiavad (The region of Kathis) viz. od, atit, satwara, saraniya, salat, sidi, jat, mahiya, dhadhi, chamtha, baloch, babar, langha, kharak, vanjara, rawal, purbiya, targala, thori, khoja, kumbhar, sanghar, sumra, sarvan, bhangi, bhopa, bhoi, luharia, limbadiya, mumna, mochi etc.

Under the influence of Islam, Kshatriyas and a tribe known as Kantiavaran shone out themselves as fighters and swordsmen. Their fighting spirit and warriors' blood have greatly influenced in shaping and molding the life of other tribes in Saurashtra as well. As a result, horse-riding, sword-playing, and art of using and manning weapons have been greatly developed by the folk of this religion. Ethos includes virtues such as faithfulness and chivalry.

All the tribes that put their feet on the soil of Gujarat since primitive times have brought with them their traditionally owned varieties of costumes and dresses of varied colors and shapes, deities-gods and goddesses, art of singing, dancing, music and even instruments, literature-folk tales and lores, customs, rituals and also festivals, beliefs, concepts of ethics and aesthetics, ways and manners of living and enjoying life including eating and drinking habits. Numerous tribes in the process of churning of the ocean, in folk creating culture have contributed what was their own and unique to make the common culture for the folk, rich and prosperous. The streams and currents thus, intermingled flowed as such that the culture today is finally the culture of the folk of Gujarat. Thus folk culture is not the outcome of efforts of an individual or a group of few people. In a way many rivers create the sea and many seas the ocean, so also it is the mixture and mingling of several tribes that created varied forms and substance of folk-culture as we have it today and all such varied aspects of various tribes have given shape to the folk culture.

To comprehend the folk-culture of gujarat, it is necessary to have awareness of its different panthakas or regions. In gujarat traditionally known as aabhirdesh-kachchha has vagad, garda, pavar, makvat, meaani, abdaso, modaso, kanthi and pranthad. In gujarat, traditionally known as aabhirdesh-kachchha has vagad, garda, pavar, makvat, meaani, abdaso, modaso, kanthi and pranthad. In kathiavad, there are okhamandal, halar, machchhu kantho, zarmario zalawad, panchal, baradi, nagher, simar, babariyawad, vadak, vagad. In naher, vadhiyar, dhandhar, chhappan, patanwada, dandhavy; khambhatbaru, bhalbaru, vankal, sankheda, mahuvan, kanthal, nimad, khandesh, mevad, raj mathor, dang, baglan, and then bhal, kaner and nalkantha of ahmedabad district. all the various tribes of these regions have developed regional culture typical to that tribe.

It is necessary to study the life of the folk in order to know the folk culture. Artistic costumes and dresses of varieties of colors and of innumerable types could be seen its folk using in Gujarat. Dresses greatly differ from caste to caste, tribes to tribes. Dresses greatly differ from caste to caste, tribes to tribes. Dresses add to the bravery of men and that which also protect. Dresses dyed in deep colors and richly embroidered clothes adorn their bodies. Together with a variety of ornaments ANAVAT-VINCHIYA, KADALA and KAMBIYU, ZUMNA, TUNPIYA, TROTIYA in different shapes add to the beauty of the bodies, both of men and women. The culture also introduced the beautifying aids such as Mehendi, Chhundana (tattoo) and Alata. Necessity brought the use of shoes, stitched and decorated artistically, to the taste of art-loving folk. This beautiful culture did not remain confined to aspects of the beautification of human bodies.

Culture of House Decoration Folk women adorned rooms and verandahs of their dwellings and houses, by rubbing the floors and plastering walls with clay mixed dung (gargormati) and Khadi (red chalkfor painting) and Okali (designing with fingers and palms, the undried mixture of clay and dung). They decorated BHINTDA(walls) with drawings and by hanging embroidered wall pieceson festivals. Their rooms beautified with madi, mand, patara,majus, kothi, and so on. Just as they adorned their kids - sonsand daughters so also for their tamed animals they stitched,sewn and embroidered colorful pieces seemly to their folk art,traditionally drawn which then continued flowing into endlessocean of folk culture.Folk Life Abounding In Folk Literature Breezes of folk-culture are there in the folk literature.The chief embodiment in this literature is their folk tales,romance, love stories, tales of chivalry, adventure anddedication, tales of Nag (cobras considered as deity), othans,tales of observance and vow, (vratas), of proverbs, sayings, oftrees, vegetation, tales of cheaters, of lakes, of ghosts, witchesand fairies and tales of horses of several kinds. Likewise in folk songs there are Garba, Garbi, Raasda, Prabhatiya or Probiya; sung on marriage ceremonies are the songs for Mandava, Mayra, Fuleka, Chori, and songs of Sanji, songs of Ukandi and Ponkhana, Fatana, Hariali songs of bride's departure after wedding; songs of sixth day of child birth, of pregnancy ceremony; and songs for Randal calling; Duhas in which there are chhakadia, Dumelia and Dodhia; lane songs Jodakana, Nachaniya and Kudaniya; Charni songs consisting of songs of seasons, ballads and heroic songs, chhandas; Adivasi songs; Bhavai songs consisting of Sorthas, Kundaliya; Rekhta and Panchakada; songs of observances and vows (vratas) Khayana, Halarda; Mourning songs consisting of Marasia, Chhajiya, Rajiya and Aaza. During procession of bride groom songs sung with longer cadence such as Saluka; Ramvada and Chandrawala sung on holi festival and Aranyu, Sarju, Savalyu sung before the goddess, Prabhati, Pad, Chopai, Sandhyaarti, Aaradhan-Stavana, Aagam, Pyala Aaambo, Barmashi, Ramgari, Dhol, Kirtan, Chadkha, Bhet, Kafi, and several others grouped in Bhajans- in all these types and kinds, there are variations from one region to the other in its contents, mode of recitations and all that; but one thing is common: the representation of feelings and emotions of the throbbing folk hearts is the same lot - the common themes, ever lively and always abounding.

The study of folk culture would not be complete unless the dialect and the colloquy - the spoken language of the folk of this region is not understood or studied. The spoken language is different at a distance of every eighteen miles-is the saying. Thus in Gujarat colloquy Sorthi, Vagadi, Charotari, Marvadi, Kachchhi, Bhili, Surati, etc. of respective regions have its own native words, proverbs, sayings and innumerable phrases with unique touchiness that characterises its folk.

Naming Humans and Animals

Naming Humans and Animals

Animal   :   Decorations

Proper nouns most prevalent among the folk have typically for instance, of the males are Rukhad, Kamlo, Ragho, Rudio, Melo, Pocho, Nagji, Vaghji, Gaghdubha, Nondhubha, Parsotam etc; of the females are Zadki, Kadvi, Savli, Daval, Jiku, Zamku, Nathi, Shivi etc. All such proper nouns are derived traditionally down to the new generations. Folk having gayful and pleasing temperament have classified their mares as Pirani, Tajan, Heman, Manki, Pati, Norali, Fulmal, Resham etc. in all thirty six types: whereas devangi horses have been termed as Chhabilo, Dhol, Chhanchhal, Reshamio etc. in all about fifteen. All types of horses account for fifty five. Cows are termed as Jambavi, Kabri, Gori, Jari, Kavli, etc. in all twenty. Kundhinyu she-buffalloes of elephant stature have been termed as Nagalyu, Bapalyu, Hetalyu etc. Bullocks classified as Makdo, Munzado, Rozdo, Khavdo, Bavdo, Dolio, Kundalo, etc. Besides names of step wells (VAV) wells, (Kuva), river, streams (Vankla), rivulets (Zara), vehicles, agricultural implements (santi) and carts (santi-gada). Tools and implements for agriculture and those of the artisans, as well as household furniture have been typically named by folk of the various regions and are worthy to be collected for a separate dictionary.Religious Observations in Folk Life Religion could also be termed as specified aspect of thefolk culture. The dominant element of religious tolerance and the sense of unity in diversities in the life lived by the folk led them to the worship of innumerable gods and goddesses and deities consisting of vegetation such as Vad, Piplo, Bordi; of creeping animals such as Nag, Nolio; of tailed animals such as Vanar (monkey, cow, crocodile and also of Surdhan (idol installed in the house) and Surapura (installed as Khambhi,). Palia-khambi indicating father-worship are of great importance.

Among deities several gods and goddesses in the folk life are static or native in origin, whereas others such as Randalma were brought in Gujarat in fourth century with the advent of Magga Parsee Barhmans throught Punjab having its dominance in the life of the folk of this soil. Each tribe has its ancestral god and goddess (Kul devta-devi) being worshipped and offered Novej at particular hours. On austere days as fixed up, with erection of Mandava; Dakla-musical instrument being played and Bhuvo (mysterious enchanter) vibrantly turning his head and arms and even body, this way and that, recites illegible words, as if to please the deity. Thus religion is tinged with devotion and blind faith in the life of the fork of all the tribes. As a normal routine, birds are served at Chabutara; flour and sugar are served to ants at Kidiyara, cows fed with grass or bread; dogs given bread and Brahmins bestowed with gifts of money, food and food grains -all this, indicative of the faith of the folk being nurtured as from olden times.

Folk Songs, Folk Dances - full of lyric Life

In fact, the folk dances are the throbbings and the spirit of the folk life of Gujarat. Among the folkdances are the Garba and Garbi of Mataji-the goddess; then Raas of Aayar, Mer, Bharvad, and Padhar; then Gheriya Raas, Dandiya Raas, Tappa, Tipani, Mashira Nritya, Matki Nritya, Ashva Nritya, Hinch, Hamchi, Titodo, Luvar and Adivasi dances need mentioning. Lok Nritya-folk dances are supported by folk music traditionally since ages. Although Bhupali, Ahir Bhairav, Pahadi and Sarang Raag have its shadows over the folk music, it is quite distinct from the classical music ever since its origin and growth.

Traditional Folk Culture & Rituals

Study of folk culture includes folk ceremonies of sacraments called sanskaras. There are in all sixteen Sanskaras. At celebrations of pregnant woman Rakhdi is tied to her wrist; on sixth day of the birth of a child, sacrament is performed and the child is named; at the age of seven to eleven, sacred thread (yagnopavit) ceremony, and ceremonies at wedding (Saptapadi) are performed as drawn out in Shastras. However the most of such ceremonies are the outcome of its observances in folk life and include ceremonies performed at death and then-after too.

Traditional Beliefs in Folk Life Omens-good and bad, faith and blind-faith, wrong beliefs and doubts do prevail in the life of the folk. While going for a good work if a dog would raise his ear, some one sneeze, snake comes across, widow comes from the front, some one would ask 'where are you going?' - these are considered as bad omens. At the hour of cowdust, the one who sleeps under 'neva' then the chariot of goddess would pass over the body; and one gets lunatic; if a child is not adorned with black spot beneath the ear, a bad sight might harm the child; if a crow speaks 'Ka, Ka' in the morning in front of the house, a guest is sure to come. Such are the beliefs and faiths traditionally prevalent among the folk.

Folk Games

Folk games are the precious gifts and assets of the folk culture. Boys, would play Moi dandia, Gedidado, Bhagdati, Aambla Pipli, Dadkidodo, Odakambli, Hadiyu, Jitvu etc. whereas girls play more interesting games and important among their games are Dedo Kutvo, Tachak Tildi, Dalo Fufufu, Tap Makhi Mara, Chaki Khande Chokla, Chalak Chalanu, Haka popatdi, Dhabu and Zabu. Grown-ups and adults play Talwar Samanavir, money on Dhol, aiming,

Padva, chopat, ghodadod (swift running), carts run, taking out branch of a tamrind tree on holi festival. Many such games among adiwasis are very well known.Folk Recipes and Dinners

Folk culture is also rich in the habits and pleasures of drinking and eating. The varieties of recipes have tastes as bitter, sour, sweet, queer, spicy, juicy, smacky, salty, sapid, flavor, savory, tanging, relishing etc. The recipes of sweets are of thirty two types and vegetable curries are of sixteen types. The dishes to serve gods are called 'Rajbhog' and to dignitaries are 'manbhog'. the most typical in folk life on important occasions are churmu and vedmi, ladva, lapsi, kansar, sukhdi, shiro, jadariyu, tal sankari etc. whereas for daily food are rotla, rotli, bhakhri, dhebra, ghensh, bodo, raab, coupled with jadariyu, kadhi, supported by pickles of keri, gajar, garmar, and papad, sarevda have importance. a poet of kathiavad has composed on bajra-rotla the typical food of ordinary folk, a nice stanza which runs as follows: "if there be bajra of mangalpur, for flour making, from dharangadhra's stone, turing wheels, clay pan prepared by didhadia's potter; dry cowdung cakes for fuel gathered from the wasteland of golasani village, And the break of day, by a house wife Having physique of a Bhimnath bull; Baked by giving very low heat, of copper color in appearance; Together with it be the curry of bringals And fresh warm milk. Even God would wish to come down to earth To enjoy this simple yet pleasant folk-food. There is also a DUHO on this : God : let thou come down to our Kathiawad, Someday perchance unknowingly; And be our guest and I bet; I would make Thee forget thy Heaven, O shamla: (Thou cloud coloured one)

The folk have a unique system at dinner. Chakla and Bajathiya for sitting and putting dishes, Dhichaniya for support to legs, Vinjanas for fanning and the host would force housewife to serve more to the guests, young, adults and elders as well. Even housewife would not herself leg behind in over-serving varieties of recipes to the guests. Here one finds how the folk culture has that noble element of hospitality unique in its own way.

Paliya - Khambhi

Palia on the periphery of every village with inscription of valor and heroics in memory of noblest of human beings are the pillars of folk civilisation. Palia not only creates history, but in itself, each of the Palia reveals its history of human behavior, full of heroic temperament that has its ethos. It is also the symbol of hero-worship. So also Khambhi erected in the memory of kin and kith speak for itself about the cherished memory of bravely departed.

Code of Conduct of Folk Culture

Thus folk culture through its ways of living, habits, customs, traditions and behaviors takes for itself a form of code of conduct. The call of the culture from the folk of Gujarat is that of hospitality, nobility, benevolence, honesty, integrity, generosity and above all character and grandeur combined to produce beauty and culture. This hereditament of greatness has not fed its folk with pleasure-seeking dullness but in fact has advocated toils and moils of hard work, noble deeds-the religion of SHRAMA and DHARMA. It speaks of 'VIJAY' Victory through Dharma. It speaks of confluence of all the religions and unity in diversities.

CHAPTER – III

TOURISM: PROBLEM AND PROSPECT

Introduction

The tourism industry is playing important role in national growth and development. Every country, every space every location has its own identity. As such, several location of Gujarat state has their own importance. Specifically the Saurashtra of Gujarat state has its unique characteristic with historical values, national beauty, commercial importance and different cultural heritage, so this topic has unique method of an inquiry and investigation.

In this research, it was decided to administer two kinds of schedules for field workers of tourism administration and travelers of Gujarat state.

[I] The survey of tourists- foreign and domestic:

This survey consist 100 respondents, who were on visit of Saurashtra region The are visitors are based from all over the country as well as abroad also. So in this reference, data have been tabulated and presented as under.

Age Wise Classification

Age gives different analytical thinking process for the person according to their preferences and response will be decided. So the researchers has taken up this factor for the analysis

AGE GROUP	Frequency	Percent
< 20	6	6.0
21 to 25	22	22.0
26 to 40	56	56.0
41 to 60	12	12.0
> 60	4	4.0
Total	100	100.0

Above table reveals the data related to the different age group of the respondents, out of 100 respondents, 6% were below 20 year, 22 percent were between 21 to 25 years, 56 percent fall 26 to 40 years age group, 12 percent fall in 41 to 60 age group and fall in 41 to 60 percent were above 60 years.

AGE

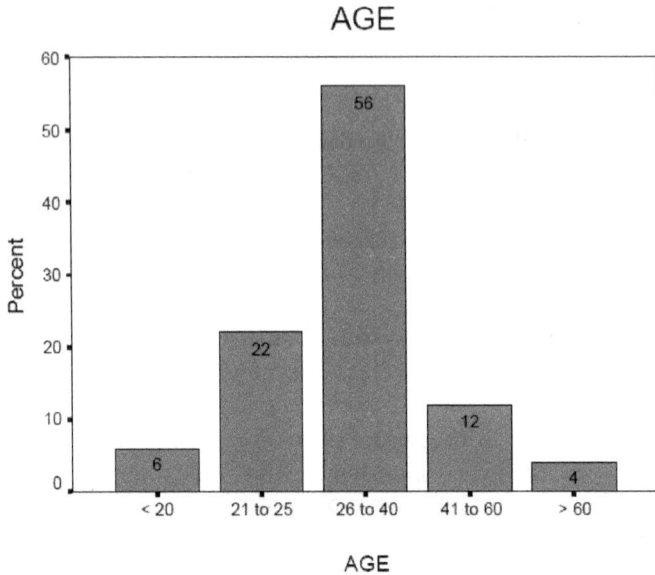

Age wise Distribution of tourists

The above table shows that the tourists have been classified on the basis of their age into five categories. The table shows that the most of the tourists i.e. 56 percent belong to the age group of 26 to 40 years, while the next 22 percent tourists were in the age group of 21 to 25 years, 12 percent tourists identified themselves with the age group of 41 to 60 years and the percentage of tourists belonging to the age group of above 60 was small i.e. only 4 percent each. Tourists upto 20 years were only 6 percent.

II Sex Wise Classification

Researcher believe that for Gujarat state, this state is popular in both the sex. There is no any gender preference, but here, there is safety, security, peace and pleasure, for journey so the family can enjoy their group and visit of several places.

Distribution of tourists according to gender

GENDER	Frequency	Percent
Male Female	51 49	51.0 49.0
Total	100	100.0

GENDER

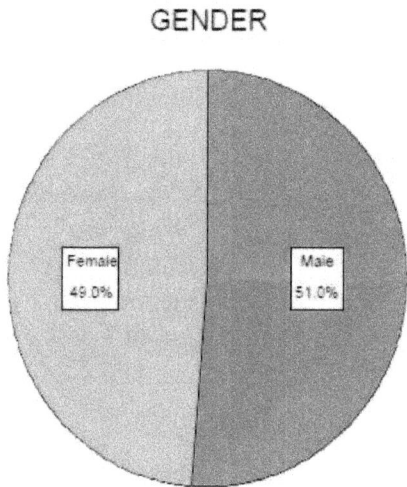

shows that out of 100 Tourists, 51 were males and 49 females. It indicates that tourism in Gujarat is slightly more popular with the males, than with the females. It was also noticed that even young women alone prefer to visit Gujarat, which means they Gujarat a relatively safe. Therefore, the female tourists prefer more outings to far places of Gujarat to have a glimpse of the old and ancient cultures.

III Family wise Classification

Family is the heart of Indian culture. The family exist in Indian culture, for love, relationship, sharing, happiness and milestone for growth. It is obvious for Indian people to move or to visit the place in group with friends and family.

Family wise Classification

Size	Frequency	Percent
2	12	12.0
3 to 4	60	60.0
5 to 6	17	17.0
7	11	11.0
Total	100	100.0

Table shows that out of 100 Tourists, 51 were males and 49 females indicate the size of the family. According to the data, out of 100 respondents, 120 respondents have visited with two family member, 60 respondents visited with 3 to4 family member, 17 percent with 5 to 6 and 11 respondents came with 7 pergons of in family.

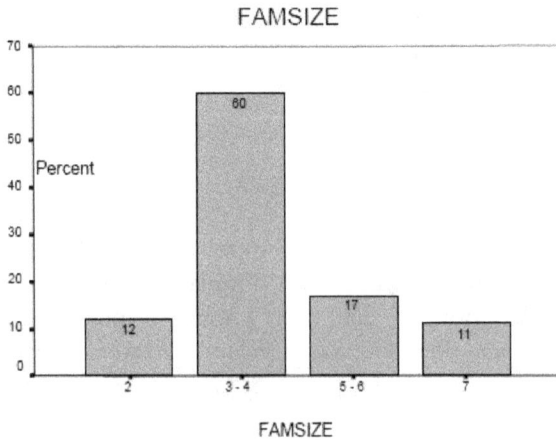

Graph Classification of tourists according to family size.

(IV) Classification accounting to the no. of accompany.

It is necessary to move or to visit place with company. In going to gather, person can share the views, pain, happiness, cove, brother hood and they enjoy the real relationship with sharing of expenses also. So the recreation has evaluated this aspect for study.

Classification of family according to accompany.

Sr. No	Classification	No	Percentage
1	Alone	34	34
2	With family	34	34
3	With friends	32	32
	Total	100	100

**Tourist's coming to Saurashtra with\
without Family\Friends**

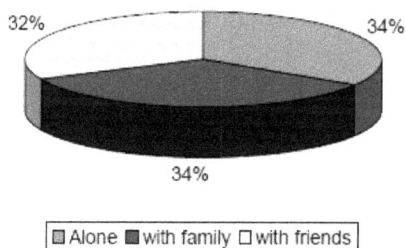

Graph: Classification of family according to accompany.

Table: shows that 34 percent of tourists came alone, while 34 percent of them visited alongwith their kids and relatives, and the remaining 32 percent arrived with their friends. The table shows that the largest numbers of tourists who belong to the age group of 20 years prefer to come alongwith their friends, and the tourists in the age group of 21-25 also choose to visit the Saurashtra usually without family but sometimes with friends. Further, it has to be noted that tourists from the age group 25 - 30 and 30 - 35 years prefer to visit alongwith their spouses while the tourists of the age group of 36 - 40 years also choose to come here alongwith their families showing that the whole family likes to enjoy the tourists trips.

V Classification according to the profession. Researcher has classified the data according to the profession. Like, business, service, farming or other. This classification is as under

Profession wise Classification

Profession	Frequency	Percent
Business	35	35.0
Service	35	35.0
Farming	20	20.0
Other	10	10.0
Total	100	100.0

Above table reveals the data of classification according to the profession, 35% belongs to business, 35% belongs to services, 20% belongs to farming and, 10 % belongs to other profession.

VI Academic qualification

Academic qualification explain the mental traits of the respondents. The various background of academic qualification may represent different understanding for tour and travel. Their preference for it, may be differ from each other. So the researcher has taken this classification with specific objective of evaluation by considering academic qualification.

Education wise Distribution of Tourists

Education	Frequency	Percent
Higher Secondary	6	6
Graduate	52	52
Post Graduate	22	22
Professional	20	20
Others	0	0
Total	100	100

The above table indicate the information about academic qualification of the respondents. Out of 100, 6 tourist were higher secondary pass, 52 were graduates, 22 were post graduates 20 were professionally qualified.

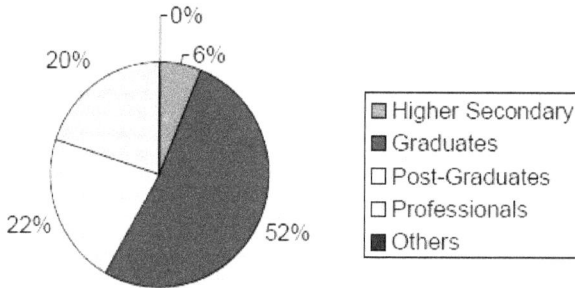

Graph Tourist Classification according to Education qualification

To identify the preferences of tourists, it is important to know their educational background. Hence, they were classified into five group like according to their educational qualifications, higher   secondary,   graduate, post-graduate, doctors and technical etc. About 6 percent H.S.C, while 22 and 20 percent each belonged to categories of post- graduates and professionals.

CHAPTER – IV

CONCLUSION AND SUGGESTIONS

There is no denying the possibility that tourism can blossom as a most prosperous smokeless and silent industry in the 21st century because it will never be a threat to ecology. Hopefully while protecting ecology, it will also generate high income especially in the form of foreign exchange. It is notable that some countries like U.K., U.S.A., Switzerland have taken special care to develop tourism on the sound basis of hotel management principles so that their consumers are fully satisfied. For that purpose, the tourism administrators in these countries have sought the help of their specialists in history, geography sociology, psychology and economic science. These specialists have helped them to evolve a perspective plan of tourism in these countries. In the Indian case the government's approach has been basically ad-hoc in nature. Not only this, in India's case tourism has been handled by rotating bureaucrats. India, it is felt, has to compete fiercely with other countries of the world in the field of tourism. There is, therefore, a need for developing a sound policy of tourism based on scientific principles of hotel management both at the National and State levels. The present state of affairs in the field of tourism is also not very heartening but still India earns more than rupees 1780 crore (1990-91) in terms of foreign currency. International bodies like the world Bank and the United Nations Economic and Social and Cultural Organisation (UNESCO) etc. are leaving no stones unturned to develop the prospects of tourism in the Third world countries.

There are, however, some danger signals from the western scholars, who argue that social, cultural and even the ecological cost of tourism is going to be heavy in the long term and therefore, long term perspective planning has to be chalked out to take care of all these factors and avoid their adverse impacts. There are complaints that many places of archaeological importance have been losing their pristine glory because of the heavy influx of tourists. Even the cultural and social attitudes of people of all such places have been affected.

Dr. M.M. Anand has done a pioneering work in this phenomenon of tourism both from managerial and strategic perspectives and dealing with the difficult task of planning and managing the tourism and hotel industry.

This study was conceived and executed in the above mentioned context to prove that a utility-oriented regional empirical study will not only help us to meet the challenges of tourism in Saurashtra - Gujarat but also contribute its humble mite to the formation of a national policy of tourism. The present study has been conducted keeping the national context in view. The study has, therefore, dealt at length not only with the governmental structures but also with non-governmental structures of tourism both at the National and State levels. Actually no State Government can develop tourism without active and enthusiastic co-operation from the national tourists structure. The need of the hour is to evolve better co-ordination between the multiple tourist structures prevalent in the country.

The first two chapters of the present study pertain to the rise and growth of tourism both in India and Saurashtra. It has been highlighted that credit goes to the Romans for the institutionalisation and commercialisation of the notions of leisure and tourism as such. India also did not lag behind. When Alexander, the great, came over to Taxila (India), he found it a prosperous centre of both trade, art and crafts.

The present work is not entirely regal, formal or institutional in nature; it is also empirical and behavioural, in its approach. For that purpose, the study incorporates responses of 100 respondents including foreigners and their responses have been analysed in the chapter of this research work. Thus, the efforts are not only normative but also empirical.

Chapterwise Summery
In the first chapter, the meaning, definition, concept and typology of tourism in the wider context of social science have been dealt with. The divergence of points of view regarding the notion of tourism itself is an indication of its being in an underdeveloped state-Gujarat. The economic, physical and social aspects must be considered before embarking on any conceptual framework of tourism. Even in the prevalent uncertainty of location, any factor motivating a visit to a destination it can be argued that there is ample scope for developing cultural tours in our Saurashtra-Gujarat in particular because of its rich cultural heritage. For that purpose places of historical and archaeological importance are to be well preserved and kept tidy. But it would be better if there is a conceptual clarity about the notion of cultural tourism before embarking on any ambitious scheme of tourism on these lines. It would be in the fitness of things if the scholars of history and archaeology were also consulted on how best we can market our rich cultural heritage in the realm of world tourism. Even the "pandits" of the Indian social reality would be of much

be initiated to define the parameters of cultural tourism alongwith its problems and prospects in the foreseeable future.

In the second chapter, tourism potentiality in the Country with its prospects and problems have been dealt with. It has been stated that this is one of the few states of India which offers many sided attraction to tourists. Its history, cultural wildlife desert, lakes, sea-sorts colourful fairs and festivals have always attracted people from all over the world to pay a visit to Gujarat. Its temples, forts, palaces, wall-paintings, architectural grandeur, art and artisans, music and dances have been instilling an urge in tourists to experience them at least once in a life time. It has been generally felt that the main bottle neck in the growth of tourism in Gujarat is the lack of comprehensive, dynamic and long-term thinking about tourism. Moreover, we must also preserve and develop some fort based human dwellings on the Williamberg pattern of the U.S.A - it has been built on the lifestyle of the 18th century and is today a popular tourist resort for European visitors. It is notable that this will not need more financial investments either because our people in village already live in the old lifestyles of the 18th and 19th centuries. Until and unless there develops better co-ordination between the various departments of the Government of Gujarat. Department of Forest, Archaeology, Temples and Tourism, Art and cultural etc. there will not be any rapid progress in the growth of this vast land of contrasts and rich cultural heritage.

The forth chapter is empirical in nature. In one category the respondents comprised the tourists both domestic and foreign.

The empirical work was completed in following ways:
The study has revealed that their exists no interdependence between variable as listed under it was found that the variables has not influence the others and these hypothesis are there fore rejected.

But it was found that the budget for purchase and family size and behaviour for purchasing and age are inter related hence these hypothesis are accepted. Thus the quantifiable variables may not be the reasons for attracting tourist to Saurashtra. Definitely ungratefully factors like historical important, natural beauty cultural aspect like dance, house decoration etc., hospitality and behaviour are the major attraction for the tourist. In order to procure tourist in Gujarat and specially Saurashtra region, sincere efforts should be made to project these aspect to the out side world through tourism development. This could be done through visual presentation of the various historical culture and religious aspect of Saurashtra and by cultural activities with participation of the local people of Saurashtra.

As regards the charges of room, meals, soft drinks, a notable feature was that the domestic tourists were critical of them and wished them to be more subsidized / economical, whereas, the foreign tourists were satisfied with the rates. The difference in judgment is obviously based on different criterion of comparison. The domestic tourists compared the rates with the domestic expenditure they incur daily on these items. Naturally, the hotel rates are much higher if so compared. However, for the foreign tourists the rates were satisfactory because they had compared them with the prevailing international rates.

In regards to the services provided like room services, transport services the reaction of both the categories of tourists was a mixed one. We also recognised the need to improve the different type of services to the national and international levels. We also have to agree to some major constraints, which are responsible for the low quality of these services in Saurashtra-Gujarat. To quote some reasons :

- Lack of finances
- Low standard of education
- Absence of training institutes leading to shortage of trained staff
- Manpower shortage
- Lack of other infrastructural facilities
- Lack of transport services
- Poor maintenance of rooms buses, buildings etc.

were additional points referred for improvements. Since a majority of tourists come for leisure and pleasure purposes more and more entertainment facilities should becreated at all the right resorts of the Gujarat Tourism Department. Also, it was felt that there is ample scope for the growth of cultural and historical tourism in the state. So it will be in the fitness of things to develop the places of historical, religious and archaeological importance. It is a fact that since tourism is an out come of the joint enterprise of several departments there should be a close collaboration between the various departments like those of forest, archaeology, temples, museums and of course, Tourism of Art and Cultural. It is also said that hotels are known outside not only because of their cuisine but also on the basis of boarding and lodging and equipped staff ought to be provided to the tourist bungalows, hotel, midways, night resorts run by the Gujarat tourism Department. There should be regular interaction between governmental and non governmental sectors of tourism and there should be some regular institutional arrangement for their meeting. There should be a close liason with both national and international tourists agencies so that foreign tourists may be tempted to visit the state of Gujarat. Since the state has to depend on the Central Government for external publicity, it must put more pressure on the center to project its image abroad vigorously. It is also felt that there should be close inter relationship between central and state tourism structures so that unnecessary overlapping and duplication may be avoided.

Suggestions

Finally suggesting the following steps to revamp the tourism administration for making tourism a grand success :

- Experts in the fields of hotel management and tourism must be associated with all the decision-making bodies of the structure.
- The Gujarat Tourism Department must have an independent research, development and analysis wing to research tourist demand and tourism structure in
- Gujarat so as to develop the prospects of tourism in the state.
- The Government of Gujarat must also develop an institute of hotel management and tourism guidance in the state to have better trained and equipped units like tourist bungalows, hotels, midways night resorts etc.
- The Government of Gujarat must open a large tourist information complex in New Delhi to motivate and guide both foreign and domestic tourists to visit the state of Gujarat.
- All the tourist information bureaus must be adequately staffed and equipped to satisfactorily perform their functions.
- Rajkot must be declared an international airport with international tourist facilities on Goa Airport so that more and more foreign tourists may be attracted to visit this state.
- Important towns of Saurashtra viz. Rajkot, Junagarh, Porbandar, Jamnagar and Surendranagar etc. should be linked with the state and national capitals by Vayudoot services.

- The state government must encourage its employees to undertake journeys providing concessions on the Central Government pattern.
- State Government should send proposals to the center for developing tourism in Gujarat and the center should provide adequate assistance to complete them. Thus the financial crunch faced by the state government would no longer hamper the development of tourism in Gujarat.
- Tourism should be declared an industry by Gujarat Government without any delay to attract the private entrepreneurs to invest in construction of hotels and other resorts.
- The State government must enact a comprehensive Tourist Act to direct and regulate the activities of the governmental and non - governmental sectors of this trade at the earliest.
- The standard of room services transport services etc. should be improved for customers' satisfaction.
- The pre-service and in-service training programmes should be started for better results.
- Promotion prospects in Gujarat Tourism Department should be improved to attract the right type of personnel.
- Better liaison should exist between State Tourism Department and ITDC.
- A state level Tourism Planning Board should be set up to do perspective planing to provide the required fillip to the tourism industry in Gujarat.

BIBLIOGRAPHY

1. Kothari C.R., Research Methodology, Wishwa Prakashan, New Delhi, 1997.
2. Sadhu Singh, Research Methodology in social science, Himalaya Publishing House, 1980.
3. O.P.Kandari, Wildlife of Garhwal Himalaya: a Recreational resource for Tourism Promotion (Srinagar, 1985) (Unpublished Doctoral Thesis, HNB Garhwal University, p.3.
4. Kim Hellen, 'An Educator's Evaluation of Tourism', PATA Report, 15th Annual Conference, san-Franscisco (California.1966), p.18
5. " 'Fair of Gujarat", Commissionerate of Information, Govt. of Gujarat, Gandhinagar.
6. " 'Gandhi Kathamruta", Kirtimandir trust, Porbandar.
7. " 'New Package Scheme of Incentives:, Department of tourism, Govt. of Gujarat 1995
8. " 'Porbandar at a Glance", Kirtimandir Trust, Porbandar.
9. " 'Tarnetar Trinetreshwar Temple", Department of archaeology, Govt. of Gujarat.
10. " 'Tourism Annual plan 97-98", Directorate of Tourism. Govt. of Gujarat, Gandhinagar.
11. " 'Wild Ass Sanctuary", Geer Foundation, Forest Department, Gujarat state 2000
12. " 'Wildlife in Gujarat", directorate of Information, Govt. of Gujarat, Gandhinagar 1997
13. S eth Pran Nath, Successful Tourism Management, Sterling Publishers Private Ltd., New Delhi 1985
14. S harma K.K., Tourism in India, classic Publishing house, Jaipur, 1991
15. S ingh P.K., Fifth years of Indian Tourism, Kanishka Publishers Publishers, New Delhi 1998
16. S ingh Ratandeep, Dynamics of Modern Tourism, Kanishka Publishers,
17. S inha P.C., Tourism Management, Anmol Publication Private Ltd., New Delhi 1998
18. Vyas Ashok, "Gujarat Darshan" Kantalaxmi Publication, Gandhinagar.